A Month of Saturdays

DOROTHY PARKER

A Month of Saturdays

Thirty-one famous pieces by
"Constant Reader"
With an Introduction
by Lillian Hellman

MACMILLAN

Contents

Contents

Contents

Contents

Publishers' Note

A column about books signed "Constant Reader" ran in *The New Yorker* almost every week from October 1927 through May 1928, and intermittently thereafter until 1933. It was an open secret that "Constant Reader" was Dorothy Parker, though her name never appeared. Her original books of poems and short stories were being published in those same years, but no one collected the Constant Reader pieces—partly, perhaps, because of the convention of pseudonymity, which would have prevented the use of her name. Yet these light-hearted essays about reading and writing played as much part in creating the Parker legend, and were as much a part of the times, as her stories and poems. They were a new and very personal kind of book reviewing. Without pretending to the Higher Criticism, they were still far from being merely fun. In the more close-knit literary world of the late twenties and early thirties, they often made or unmade reputations. And time has confirmed most of her judgments.

Of the forty-six Constant Reader pieces that appeared, thirty-one have been reprinted here in whole or in part. We have chosen to present them in the mood and manner of their original appearance—without editing except for indicated cuts. Constant Reader did not need to remind her readers who the authors were and what they had written before. Most of the writers she chose, whether to praise or to stick pins in, were literary figures of the day, and their names were on everyone's lips. When they were less known, she explained them sufficiently in her article. Nor did she need to identify people she mentioned in passing, such as President Lowell, or Elwell, or Geraldine Farrar. Their names were symbols. For younger readers a few notes have been supplied at the end of the pieces to which they apply.

This selection could not have been made without the advice and consent of Miss Lillian Hellman, Dorothy Parker's executrix. Miss Hellman, however, graciously deferred to the Viking editors when differences of opinion arose, and she bears no responsibility for the final collection. The publishers express their gratitude to her, and also to *The New Yorker,* for their willingness to have Constant Reader now appear in book form for the first time.

INTRODUCTION
by *Lillian Hellman*

I first met Dorothy Parker in 1931, shortly after I moved back to New York with Hammett. She caused a wacky-tipsy fight between us. She had read *The Maltese Falcon* and *Red Harvest*, perhaps a year or two before, and she had written about them, but she had not met Hammett until a cocktail party given by William Rose Benét. I was already uncomfortable at this party of people much older than myself, when a small, worn, prettyish woman was introduced to Hammett and immediately fell to her knees before him and kissed his hand. It was meant to be both funny and serious, but it was neither, and Hammett was embarrassed into a kind of simper.

I had a habit in those days—there are still often hangovers of it on other levels—of making small matters into large symbols and, after enough cocktails, I saw the gesture as what New York life was going to be like for an unknown young woman among the famous. That night I accused Dash of liking ladies who kissed his hand, he said I was crazy, I said I wasn't going to live with a man who allowed women to kneel in admiration, he said he had "allowed" no such thing, didn't like it, but if I wanted to leave right away, he would not detain me. I said I'd go as soon as I had finished my steak, but I guess by that time we were fighting about something else, because a few months later he said if I ever reminded him of the incident again, I would never live to finish another steak.

I was not to meet Dottie again until the winter of 1935 in Hollywood, and then, having glared at her for most of the evening in memory of that silly first meeting, we talked. I liked her and we saw each other the next day and for many, many other good days and years until she died in June of 1967.

It was strange that we did like each other and that never through the years did two such difficult women ever have a quarrel, or even a mild, unpleasant word. Much, certainly, was against our friendship: we were not the same generation, we were not the same kind of writer, we had led and were to continue to lead very different lives, often we didn't like the same people or even the same books, but more important, we never liked the same men. When I met her in 1935 she was married to Alan Campbell, who was a hard man for me to take. He was also difficult for her and she would talk about him in a funny, half-bitter way not only to me but given enough liquor, to a whole dinner party. But she had great affection for Alan and certainly—since she was to marry him twice—great dependence on him. If I didn't like Alan, she didn't like Hammett, although she was always too polite to say so. More important to me, Hammett, who seldom felt strongly about anybody, didn't like Dottie, and in the later years would move away from the house when she came to visit us. He was not conscious that his face would twist, almost as if he had half recovered from a minor stroke, as she embraced and flattered a man or woman, only to turn, when they had left the room, to say in the soft, pleasant, clear voice, "Did you ever meet such a shit?" I think the game of embrace-denounce must have started when she found it amused or shocked people, because in time, when she found it didn't amuse me, she seldom played it. But Hammett found it downright distasteful and I gave up all efforts to convince him that it was the kind of protection sometimes needed by those who are frightened.

I am no longer certain that I was right: fear now seems too simple. The game more probably came from a desire to charm, to be loved, to be admired, and such desires brought self-contempt that could only be consoled by behind-the-back denunciations of almost comic violence.

If she denounced everybody else, I had a right to think that I was included, but now I think I was wrong about that, too: so many people have told me that she never did talk about me, never complained, never would allow gossip about me, that I have come to believe it. But even when I didn't, it didn't matter. I enjoyed her more than I have ever enjoyed any other woman. She was modest—this wasn't all virtue, she liked to think that she was not worth much—her view of people was original and sharp, her elaborate, over-delicate manners made her a pleasure to live with, she liked books and was generous about writers, and the wit, of course, was so wonderful that neither age nor illness ever dried up the spring from which it came fresh each day. No remembrance of her can exclude it.

The joke has been changed and variously

attributed to Mischa Elman and Heifetz, but it is hers, because I was there when it happened. We were knitting before the living room fireplace in the country house that she and Alan once owned in Pennsylvania. Upstairs, Alan was having an argument with his visiting mother. The afternoon grew dark, it began to snow, we made the fire very large and sat in silence. Occasionally, the upstairs voices would grow angry loud and then Dottie would sigh. When the voices finally ceased, Alan appeared in the living room.

He said, immediately, angrily, "It's hot as hell in here."

"Not for orphans," Dottie said, and I laughed for so long that Alan went for a walk and Dottie patted my hand occasionally and said, "There, there, dear, you'll choke if you're not careful."

Once she said to me—I quoted it at her funeral and found to my pleasure, as it would have been to hers, that the mourners laughed—"Lilly, promise me that my gravestone will carry only these words: 'If you can read this you've come too close.'"

Long before I knew her she dined in Paris with a group of Lesbians who were seriously talking of the possibility of legal marriage between them. Dottie listened most politely, clucked in agreement. They expected her friendly opinion and asked for it. The large eyes were wide with sympathy. "Of course you must have legal marriages. The children have to be considered."

But for me, the wit was never as attractive as the comment, often startling, always sudden, as if a curtain had opened and you had a brief and brilliant glance into what you would never have found for yourself. Like the wit, it was always delivered in a soft, clear voice; like the wit, it usually came after a silence, and started in the middle. One day she looked up from a book: "The man said he didn't want to see her again. That night she tried to climb into the transom of his hotel room and got stuck at the hips. I've never got stuck at the hips, Lilly, and I want you to remember that."

Dottie was very fond of the Gerald Murphys, but fondness never had anything to do with judgment. The Murphys had been in Europe and she had not seen them for six or eight months. We met to walk to their apartment for dinner. Dottie said, "Make a guess who Gerald will have discovered this time, what writer, I mean."

I said I couldn't guess, I didn't know Gerald as well as she did.

She said, "O.K. Give me three guesses and if I hit one right, will you buy me a drunken lunch tomorrow?"

I agreed and she said immediately, "Madame de Staël, Gerard Manley Hopkins or Philippe de Swarzberger."

"Who is Philippe de Swarzberger?"

"An Alsatian who moved around Tibet. Born 1837, died 1871, or so it's thought. A mystic, most of whose work has been lost, but two volumes remain in Lausanne under lock and key, and Gerald invented him this afternoon."

We had a fine dinner at the Murphys and were drinking our brandy when Gerald produced a small book and asked if he could read a few poems from it. It was, indeed, a volume of Gerard Manley Hopkins.

It was Gerald who told the story that always seemed to me to sum up the contradictions in the Parker nature. Long before I met her, she had an affair of high tragi-comedy with a handsome, rich, wellborn stockbroker, getting extra enjoyment from it because Elinor Wylie had also had her eye on him. Murphy said that one night he called to take Dottie to dinner. She appeared as neat and pretty as usual, but with a black eye, recently caked blood on the mouth, and nasty bruises on the arm. She explained to Gerald that the well-born had beaten her up the night before, that even worse cuts and bruises were concealed by her dress.

Gerald, horrified, said, "How can you bear that man, Dottie? He's a very dirty cad."

Dottie turned to stare at him, opened the door of the taxi, said softly, "I can't let you talk about him that way, Gerald," and fell from the taxi into the middle of Park Avenue traffic. (The cad, many years and a wife or two later, was to fire a gun into his mouth in the Martha's Vineyard airport.)

Her taste in men was, indeed, bad, even for writer ladies. She had been loved by several remarkable men, but she only loved the ones who did not love her, and they were the shabby ones. Robert Benchley had loved her, I was told by many people, and certainly I was later to see the devotion he had for her and she for him. She had had an affair with Ring Lardner, and both of these men she respected, and never attacked—a rare mark of feeling—but I don't think she was in love with them, because respect somehow cancelled out romantic love. (She talked far too much about how men looked—handsome, well-made, and so on.) But then her relations with lovers, and with her husband, were always a mystery to me—perhaps because I had missed the early days of the attempted suicides, the long, famous tape of the broken heart. There is no question she wanted it that way—she wanted the put-down from everybody and anybody, and she always resented it and hit back. The pride was very great, although she never recognized that she so often pleaded for the indignity that offended it.

But she was, more than usual, a tangled fishnet of contradictions: she liked the rich because she liked the way they looked, their clothes, the things in their houses, and she disliked them with an open and baiting contempt; she believed in socialism but seldom, except in the sticky sentimental minutes, could stand the sight of a working radical; she drank far too much, spent far too much time with ladies who did, and made fun of them and herself every inch of the way; she faked interest and sympathy for those who bored her and for whom she had no feeling, and yet I never heard her hit mean except where it was, in some sense, justified; she herself was frightened of being hit, being made fun of, being inconvenienced, yet when she was called by the House Un-American Activities Committee and I went to say that I would come with her, she said, in genuine surprise, "Why, Lilly?" I don't think it occurred to her, or to many of her generation, that the ruling classes were anything but people with more money than you had. She acted before the committee as she acted so often with their more literate, upper-class cousins at dinner: as if to say, "Yes, dear, it's true that I'm here to observe you, but I do not like you and will, of course, say and write exactly that."

But she wrote it too often in sentimental short stories about the little dressmaker or the servant as they are patronized by the people Dottie had dined with the night before. It was her way of paying back the rich and powerful, and if it is understandable in life it is too raw and unshaded for literature. The good short stories, like "Big Blonde," are her imaginative projections of what she knew or feared for herself, and have nothing to do with vengeance on the rich. Her put-them-in-their-place stories are often undigested, the conclusions there on the first page. The other stories, and much of the light verse, I think, are a valuable record of their time and place.

But I am not an intelligent critic of those I like. It is not that I am overgenerous or overloyal, it's that their work, from the very best to the not very good, is too close to what I know about them, or hope to find out, and thus I am so occupied by the revelations of the author in the work that I cannot be cool about the work itself. This has been of value: it has made it possible to be good friends with writers who, in the end, do not require extravagant praise if you make clear that you have little interest in extravagant analysis. A book is good, bad or medium for me, and I usually don't know the reasons why. Years later, I will often think the good was not as good as I once thought, but on the record, my inability to know the why, my rather lumpish, incoherent acceptance or rejection, has often been less mistaken than those who care more or know more of what literature is made.

And so it was with Dottie. I never gave her all the good words she got from so many others, and I always cut off her praise of my work, never sure that she meant it, never really caring. We were polite, we were reticent, but very little fakery was given or required, although certainly we both lied now and then about each other's work and we both knew it. I once wrote a short story, my first since I was very young, and gave it to her to read. She had warm words for it, but the fact that she picked up a phrase—I no longer remember what phrase—and kept praising its originality and delicacy, worried me. A few months later she asked me what I had done with the story. I said I had decided it was a lady-writer story, not about anything. She protested, she quoted the phrase again, she said how much impressed she had been, and she tripped over a group of poodle puppies that we had brought along on our walk. As she stooped down to console them, I said, "God is not just. He punishes puppies for the lies of pretty ladies to their friends."

She said, "Lilly, I do like the story"—but I had walked ahead of her.

In a few minutes she caught up with me and we went in silence to the lake. It was a cold spring, but Hammett and I had decided to set the snapping turtle traps earlier than usual and I was anxious to have a look at them. I hauled up one of the long, wire cages and there was our first turtle of the year. As I put the cage on the ground to look at him, his penis extended in fear.

Dottie said, "It must be pleasant to have sex appeal for turtles. Shall I leave you alone together?" She had paid me back and all was well.

After Dottie married Alan Campbell for the second time—she had phoned me from California immediately after the wedding reception with "Lilly, the room was filled with people who hadn't talked to each other in years, including the bride and bridegroom"—we did not see each other as often as in the years before. But there would be periods when she moved back to New York and would come to stay with me in Martha's Vineyard. It was in those years that Dash would pack and leave the house to return only after Dottie had left. But there was the last painful summer of his life when he couldn't leave any place any more and I had to lie to Dottie about the reason for putting her up in a guest house down the road. I would sit with Dash as he nibbled on his early dinner and pretend to eat from my tray. Almost immediately he would sleep from the weariness of eating, and Dottie would come soon after to have dinner with me. I never ate a whole dinner that summer, partly because the pretend eating had spoiled my appetite, partly because I was so often silent angry with Hammett for making the situation hard for me, not knowing then that the dying do not, should not, be asked to think about anything but their own minute of running time. Dottie stayed about a month that year without ever seeing Dash, and the measure of her tact was that she never asked a question about a situation she must have understood.

Hammett died that next winter, I sold the Vineyard house, and built myself a new house. The first telephone call in the new house came from Dottie to tell me that Alan was dead from an overdose of sleeping pills. She was very sure that the overdose was not intentional—she believed he had had too much to drink and had forgotten how many pills he had taken. I believed her. Alan was the first person I ever knew to take sleeping pills and I remember a trip to Europe the three of us made on the old *Normandie*.

One day I said to Dottie, "What happens to Alan every afternoon, where is he?"

"Takes a sleeping pill. He hates to toss and turn from four to six."

Less than a year after Alan's death, Dottie moved back to New York. We saw each other, of course, but after the first few times I knew I could not go back to the past. The generation difference between us seemed shorter as I grew older, but I was irritable now with people who drank too much and Dottie's drinking made her dull and repetitive, and she made me sad. I had money again but no longer enough to give it without thought before it was needed, which is the way it used to be between us; but mainly, plainly, I did not want the burdens that Dottie, maybe by never asking for anything, always put upon her friends. I was tired of trouble and wanted to be around people who walked faster than I and might pull me along with them.

And so, for the next five years of her life, I was not the good friend I had been. True, I was there in emergencies, but I was out the door immediately they were over. I found that Dottie's middle age, old age, made rock of much that had been fluid, and eccentricities once charming become too strange for safety or comfort.

Dottie had always, even in the best days, clung

to the idea that she was poor. Often she was, because she was generous to others and to herself, but more often it came from an insistence on a world where the artist was the put-upon outsider, the *épaté* rebel who ate caviar from rare china with a Balzac shrug for when you paid. I had long ago given up trying to figure out her true poverty periods from the pretend-poverty periods, and the last sick years seemed no time to argue. She had, many years before, given me a Picasso gouache and a Utrillo landscape, saying as she gave them that she was leaving them to me anyway, so why not have them now? It was her charming way of paying off a debt and I remember being impressed with the grace. A few years after the gift, when I thought she was short of money, I sold the Utrillo and sent her a check. (She never told me that she had received the check, we never spoke of it at all.) Now, in 1965, she needed money and so I decided to sell the Picasso. It was a good, small picture, sold immediately for ten thousand dollars, and I took the check to Dottie the day I got it. Two days later, a woman unknown to me phoned to say that Dottie was in the hospital, sick and without money. I said that couldn't be, she said it was, and would I guarantee the hospital bills? I went to the hospital that day. Dottie and I talked for a long time, and as I rose to go I said, "Dottie, do you need money?"

"She's been calling you," she said, "the damned little meddler. She's called half of New York to make me into a pleading beggar."

"She meant no harm. She thinks you're broke."

"I *am* broke, Lilly. But I don't want people, not even you—"

"You're not broke. I gave you a check two days ago for ten thousand dollars. Where is it?"

She stared at me and then turned her face away. She said, very softly, "I don't know."

And she didn't know, she was telling the truth. She wanted to be without money, she wanted to forget she had it. The check was found in a bureau drawer along with three other checks. It had always been like that, it always would be. After her death, and nobody ever left fewer accumulations, I found four uncashed seven-year-old checks. She never had much, but what she had she didn't care about, and that was very hat-over-the-windmill stuff in a sick lady of seventy-four.

What money she had, she left to Martin Luther King, a man she had never met. I was the only executor of the will. I was, I am, moved that she wanted it that way, because the will had been dictated during the years of my neglect. But I had always known and always admired her refusal to chastise or complain about neglect. When, in those last years, I would go for a visit she always had the same entrance speech for me, "Oh, Lilly, come in quick. I want to laugh again." In the same circumstances, I would have said, "Where have you been?"

And in a little while, we would laugh again, not as often, not as loud as in the old days, but enough to give us both a little of the old pleasure. Her wit, of course, was delicate, clear, and sharp. I don't know what mine is, but it isn't that, and I never knew why it amused her. But we were affectionate about each other's jokes, even when they weren't very good, and would endlessly repeat them to other people with the pride of mothers. (She never in her life repeated her own witticisms, perhaps sure that other people would do it for her. I was one of the many who did.)

Even now I don't think of her as dead, and only a few weeks ago, when Peter Feibleman told me a story I had not heard before, I had a nice minute of wanting to reach for the telephone. The story is all of her as age put aside the deceits of youth, as time solidified the courage she didn't want to admit was there.

Feibleman was with her when Alan Campbell's body was taken to the coroner's car. (No charge of suicide was ever made.) Among the friends who stood with Dottie on those California steps was Mrs. Jones, a woman who had liked Alan, had pretended to like Dottie, and who had always loved all forms of meddling in other people's troubles. Mrs. Jones said, "Dottie, tell me, dear, what I can do for you."

Dottie said, "Get me a new husband."

There was a silence, but before those who would have laughed could laugh, Mrs. Jones said, "I think that is the most callous and disgusting remark I ever heard in my life."

Dottie turned to look at her, sighed, and said gently, "So sorry. Then run down to the corner and get me ham and cheese on rye and tell them to hold the mayo."

A Month of Saturdays

The Private Papers of the Dead

I think that the *Journal of Katherine Mansfield* ¶
is the saddest book I have ever read. Here, set
down in exquisite fragments, is the record of six
lonely and tormented years, the life's-end of a des-
perately ill woman. So private is it that one feels
forever guilty of prying for having read it.

Her journal was her dear companion. "Come,
my unseen, my unknown, let us talk together,"
she says to it. Only in its pages could she show
her tragically sensitive mind, her lovely, quivering soul. She was not of the little breed of the dis-
contented; she was of the high few fated to be ever
unsatisfied. Writing was the precious thing in life
to her, but she was never truly pleased with anything she had written. With a sort of fierce aus-
terity, she strove for the crystal clearness, the hard,
bright purity from which streams perfect truth.
She never felt that she had attained them.

This is the book of a writer. Not, I mean, that
there are chummy bits of "literary gossip" or
John-Farrar-like anecdotes of the bookmen of ¶
her acquaintance. But Katherine Mansfield could
look on at herself, so to say, and see even in her
physical sufferings material for her pen. "I must
remember it," she says, after a racking agony of

lumbago, "when I write about an old man." "Let me remember," she prays of a smoky rain, a violin note, a shiny, blue day. There are plans for stories —so many that she did not live to carry out—and sketches of characters. These are not set down in the dreadful manner of the two-story-a-week writers who carry obnoxious notebooks about, snapping at "copy." She wrote them in her journal, this journal that was for her alone, because here was her life, because the writer and the woman were not and could never be two separate beings.

The photographs of her that illustrate the journal are of deep interest. The first was taken in 1913; the last shortly before her death ten years later. She grew always more beautiful for her suffering.

Journal of Katherine Mansfield is a beautiful book and an invaluable one, but it is her own book, and only her dark, sad eyes should have read its words. I closed it with a little murmur to her portrait on the cover. "Please forgive me," I said.

October 8, 1927

¶ Katherine Mansfield (1888–1923), the short-story writer, was the wife of John Middleton Murry, the English critic. When he published her private journals after her death, some felt that he was exploiting her. . . . John Farrar (1896–), publisher and patron of young writers, was editor of *The Bookman,* a literary monthly of the time.

An American Du Barry

Nan Britton, the author of the American classic, *The President's Daughter*, affirms that she wrote her book solely as a plea for more civilized laws affecting the standing of the children of unmarried mothers. And maybe she did. And maybe the writer of "Only a Boy" set down that tale just for the purpose of arousing interest in bigger and better crèches.

The President's Daughter is the most amazing work that has yet found its way into these jittering hands. It is the story of the affair between Nan Britton and Warren Gamaliel Harding; and Miss Britton takes you through their romance in a glass-bottomed boat, as it were. The book bears the subtitle *Revealing the Love-Secret of President Harding*, which is but a mild statement. For when Miss Britton gets around to revealing, Lord, how she does reveal. She is one who kisses, among other things, and tells.

An attempt was made to suppress the book. The author states, in one of her prefaces, that "six burly policemen" (on the day that that man bites that dog, another front-page item is going to concern a policeman who is not burly) "and John S. Sumner, agent for the Society for the Suppression of Vice, armed with a 'Warrant of Search and Seizure,' entered the printing plant where the making of the book was in process. They seized and carried off the plates and printed sheets." "Lady," you want to say to the author, "those weren't policemen; they were critics of literature dressed up." I admit I drank down the whole book; but one swallow would make a Sumner. (That should have been better. I wish I had more time. Something might have been made of that.)

However, "in a magistrate's court the case was dismissed. The seized plates and printed sheets were returned to the publishers—the Elizabeth Ann Guild, Inc." So now the whole literate world may have the privilege of reading, at five dollars a crack, of the indoor life of the mighty.

Of the authenticity of Miss Britton's story I am absolutely convinced. I wish I were not. I wish I could feel that she had made it all up out of her head, for then I could give myself over to high ecstasies at the discovery of the great American satire, the shrewd and savage critique of Middle-Western love. But I am afraid that *The President's Daughter* is only a true story.

Throughout her book, Miss Britton protests, perhaps a shade too much, of the great love that she and Mr. Harding bore each other, a love which she insists, in a phrase that I am fairly sure I have seen before some place, could not have been greater had they been joined together by fifty ministers; yet they seem to have been, at best, but a road-company Paolo and Francesca. Theirs is the tale of as buckeye a romance as you will find. It is, and a hundred per cent, an American comedy.

The one faint glimpse of glamour that Miss Britton allows us is that of her early days, when she had a little-girl's crush on the Marion editor, more than thirty years her senior, who was just stepping off into politics. Then she sees him as a truly romantic figure, in all he does and says, as, for instance, on that memorable day when her mother "allowed me to go up and shake hands with him and tell him how much I enjoyed his speech, for which hesitating utterance I received one of his loveliest smiles and a courtly 'Thank you kindly, thank you kindly!' "

But when she has grown up into his extramural affections, she seems to view him as someone a little less than glamorous. "Between kisses," she says, "we found time to discuss my immediate need for a position." She tells you of the time when, in alighting from a taxi in front of the Manhattan Hotel, "Mr. Harding caught his foot and tripped, falling in a very awkward position. . . . Mr. Harding's blush of confusion after his fall remained a good many minutes and was explained by him, 'You see, dearie, I'm so crazy about you that I don't know where I'm stepping!' " She speaks of his tucking thirty dollars in her brand new silk stocking. She relates of his hiding in the cupboard when there was an unexpected knock upon the door of her apartment. She tells you about that afternoon when the house detective put them firmly though gently out of an hotel room, despite his plea that they weren't disturbing any of the other guests. " 'Gee, Nan,' was Our President's comment upon that occasion, 'I thought I wouldn't get out of that under a thousand dollars!' "

Mr. Harding, one gathers, was scarcely of the drunken-sailor temperament. He paid five dollars a pair for his shoes and announced that "That is all any fellow should pay for shoes." When his bill for a dinner was over fifteen dollars, "Mr. Harding tipped the waiter $1.50. I watched his face as he counted out the money. . . . He looked across at me and shrugged his shoulders. 'You know, Nan, I am not penurious, but a bill like that is really ridiculous.' " He took Miss Britton to the theatre, and chivalrously begged her to guess what he paid for the tickets; the correct answer turned out to be $5.50 apiece. "War-time graft" he termed this. One can but feel, after several of these anecdotes, that Miss Britton was doing admirably to get that thirty dollars tucked into her stocking.

Nor was he precisely a poetic lover. "Dearie" was his most flowery term, and sometimes "to show me he was really just human like myself, he would deliberately use words like 'ain't' " or call his lady "you purty thing!" The shy Miss Britton, because of the difference in their ages, could not quite bring herself to call him Warren; she compromised on "sweetheart."

Surely this story of so bare and shabby a love, of these meetings held in hotels recommended by taxi drivers, and, some time after the man had been made President of the United States, of that tryst in a clothes closet, should be a pathetic thing. But so smug is Miss Britton's style, so sure of himself does she make Harding appear, that one can look on this affair only as a comic, and a slightly horrid, matter. There was no wistfulness in either the practical young lady or her pompous lover.

For the unfortunate little Elizabeth Ann, the child of Nan Britton and Warren Gamaliel Harding, one can only wish that no one will show her this book that so unbeautifully exploits her. Undoubtedly, it will make money, and, one trusts, for her. It is lofty on the list of best sellers, despite the fact that it is allowed no advertising. Probably it will become a greater popular favorite than *We*. This is, you remember, America.

October 15, 1927

Re-enter Margot Asquith—A Masterpiece from the French

"Daddy, what's an optimist?" said Pat to Mike while they were walking down the street together one day.

¶ "One who thought that Margot Asquith wasn't going to write any more," replied the absent-minded professor, as he wound up the cat and put the clock out.

That gifted entertainer, the Countess of Oxford and Asquith, author of *The Autobiography of Margot Asquith* (four volumes, neatly boxed, suitable for throwing purposes), reverts to tripe in a new book deftly entitled *Lay Sermons*. It is a little dandy if I have ever seen one, and I certainly have.

I think it must be pleasanter to be Margot Asquith than to be any other living human being; and this is no matter of snap judgment on my part, for I have given long and envious thought ¶ to the desirability of being Charles A. Levine. But the lady seems to have even more self-assurance than has the argumentative birdman. Her perfect confidence in herself is a thing to which monuments should be erected; hers is a poise that ought to be on display in the British Museum. The affair between Margot Asquith and Margot Asquith will live as one of the prettiest love stories in all literature.

In this book of essays, which has all the depth and glitter of a worn dime, the Countess walks right up to such subjects as Health, Human Nature, Fame, Character, Marriage, Politics, and Opportunities. A rather large order, you might say, but it leaves the lady with unturned hair. Successively, she knocks down and drags out each topic. And there is something vastly stirring in the way in which, no matter where she takes off from, she brings the discourse back to Margot Asquith. Such singleness of purpose is met but infrequently.

When she does get around to less personal matters, it turns out that her conclusions are soothingly far from startling. A compilation of her sentiments, suitably engraved upon a nice, big calendar, would make an ideal Christmas gift for your pastor, your dentist, or Junior's music teacher. Here, for instance, are a few ingots lifted from her golden treasury: "The artistic temperament has been known to land people in every kind of dilemma." . . . "Pleasure will always make a stronger appeal than Wisdom." . . . "It is only the fine natures that profit by Experience." . . . "It is better to be a pioneer than a passenger, and best of all to try and create." . . . "It is not only what you See but what you Feel that kindles appreciation and gives life to Beauty." . . . "Quite apart from the question of sex, some of the greatest rascals have been loved." . . . "I think it is a duty women owe not only to themselves, but to everyone else, to dress well."

The Thames, I hear, remains as damp as ever in the face of these observations.

Through the pages of *Lay Sermons* walk the great. I don't say that Margot Asquith actually permits us to rub elbows with them ourselves, but she willingly shows us her own elbow, which has been, so to say, honed on the mighty. "I remember President Wilson saying to me"; "John Addington Symonds once said to me"; "The Master of Balliol told me"—thus does she introduce her anecdotes. And you know those anecdotes that begin that way; me, I find them more efficacious than sheep-counting, rain on a tin roof, or alanol tablets. Just begin a story with such a phrase as "I remember Disraeli—poor old Dizzy! —once saying to me, in answer to my poke in the eye," and you will find me and Morpheus off in a corner, necking.

Margot Asquith's is, I am sure, a naïve and an annoying (those two adjectives must ever be synonyms to me) and an unimportant book, yet somehow, grudge it though I do, there is a disarming quality to it and to its author. (There I go, getting tender about things, again; it's no wonder men forget me.) Perhaps it is because the lady's cocksureness implies a certain sort of desperate gallantry; perhaps it is because there is a little—oh, entirely unconscious, please, Your Grace—wistfulness in the recurrent references to the dear dead days of "The Souls," in the tales of the hunting-field when the high gentry were wont to exclaim, "You ride with such audacity, Miss Tennant!" I suppose that wistfulness is a fighting word to the Countess, but there it stands. She is, from her book, no master mind, God wot; but she is, also from her book, a game woman, gamer, I think, than she knows. I always have to cry a little bit about courage.

However (and how good it feels to get back to the nice, firm ground again), *Lay Sermons* is a naïve and an annoying and an unimportant book. The author says, "I am not sure that my ultimate choice for the name of this modest work is altogether happy." Happier I think it would have been if, instead of the word "Sermons," she had selected the word "Off."

The Counterfeiters is too tremendous a thing for ¶ praises. To say of it "Here is a magnificent novel" is rather like gazing into the Grand Canyon and remarking, "Well, well, well; quite a slice."

Doubtless you have heard that this book is not pleasant. Neither, for that matter, is the Atlantic Ocean.

October 22, 1927

¶ MARGOT (TENNANT) ASQUITH (1864–1945), wife of the British Prime Minister of 1908–1916, was known as a wit in London literary and social circles. . . . CHARLES A. LEVINE made headlines in 1927 by following a few days after Lindbergh in a nonstop transatlantic flight, with Clarence D. Chamberlain, which overshot Berlin. . . . *The Counterfeiters* was so much talked about on publication that Constant Reader did not need to mention the name of the author: ANDRÉ GIDE (1869–1951), French writer and intellectual, who later won the Nobel Prize.

A Book of Great Short Stories

Ernest Hemingway wrote a novel called *The Sun Also Rises*. Promptly upon its publication, Ernest Hemingway was discovered, the Stars and Stripes were reverentially raised over him, eight hundred and forty-seven book reviewers formed themselves into the word "welcome," and the band played "Hail to the Chief" in three concurrent keys. All of which, I should think, might have made Ernest Hemingway pretty reasonably sick.

For, a year or so before *The Sun Also Rises,* he had published *In Our Time,* a collection of short pieces. The book caused about as much stir in literary circles as an incompleted dogfight on upper Riverside Drive. True, there were a few that went about quick and stirred with admiration for this clean, exciting prose, but most of the reviewers dismissed the volume with a tolerant smile and the word "stark." It was Mr. Mencken who slapped it down with "sketches in the bold, bad manner of the Café du Dôme," and the smaller boys, in their manner, took similar pokes at it. Well, you see, Ernest Hemingway was a young American living on the left bank of the Seine in Paris, France; he had been seen at the Dôme and the Rotonde and the Select and the Closerie des Lilas. He knew Pound, Joyce, and Gertrude Stein. There is something a little—well, a little *you-*

know—in all of those things. You wouldn't catch
Bruce Barton or Mary Roberts Rinehart doing ¶
them. No, sir.

And besides, *In Our Time* was a book of short
stories. That's no way to start off. People don't
like that; they feel cheated. Any bookseller will
be glad to tell you, in his interesting *argot,* that
"short stories don't go." People take up a book
of short stories and say, "Oh, what's this? Just a lot
of those short things?" and put it right down again.
Only yesterday afternoon, at four o'clock sharp, I
saw and heard a woman do that to Ernest Hemingway's new book, *Men Without Women.* She had
been one of those most excited about his novel.

Literature, it appears, is here measured by a
yard-stick. As soon as *The Sun Also Rises* came
out, Ernest Hemingway was the white-haired boy.
He was praised, adored, analyzed, best-sold, ar-
gued about, and banned in Boston; all the trim-
mings were accorded him. People got into feuds
about whether or not his story was worth the
telling. (You see this silver scar left by a bullet,
right up here under my hair? I got that the night
I said that any well-told story was worth the telling. An eighth of an inch nearer the temple, and
I wouldn't be sitting here doing this sort of tripe.)
They affirmed, and passionately, that the dissolute
expatriates in this novel of "a lost generation"
were not worth bothering about; and then they
devoted most of their time to discussing them.
There was a time, and it went on for weeks, when
you could go nowhere without hearing of *The
Sun Also Rises.* Some thought it without excuse;
and some, they of the cool, tall foreheads, called
it the greatest American novel, tossing *Huckle-*

berry Finn and *The Scarlet Letter* lightly out the window. They hated it or they revered it. I may say, with due respect to Mr. Hemingway, that I was never so sick of a book in my life.

Now *The Sun Also Rises* was as "starkly" written as Mr. Hemingway's short stories; it dealt with subjects as "unpleasant." Why it should have been taken to the slightly damp bosom of the public while the (as it seems to me) superb *In Our Time* should have been disregarded will always be a puzzle to me. As I see it—I knew this conversation would get back to me sooner or later, preferably sooner—Mr. Hemingway's style, this prose stripped to its firm young bones, is far more effective, far more moving, in the short story than in the novel. He is, to me, the greatest living writer of short stories; he is, also to me, not the greatest living novelist.

After all the high screaming about *The Sun Also Rises,* I feared for Mr. Hemingway's next book. You know how it is—as soon as they all start acclaiming a writer, that writer is just about to slip downward. The littler critics circle like literary buzzards above only the sick lions.

So it is a warm gratification to find the new Hemingway book, *Men Without Women,* a truly magnificent work. It is composed of thirteen short stories, most of which have been published before. They are sad and terrible stories; the author's enormous appetite for life seems to have been somehow appeased. You find here little of that peaceful ecstasy that marked the camping trip in *The Sun Also Rises* and the lone fisherman's days in "Big Two-Hearted River" in *In Our Time.* The stories include "The Killers," which seems to me one of the four great American short stories. (All you have to do is drop the nearest hat, and I'll tell you what I think the others are. They are Wilbur Daniel Steele's "Blue Murder," Sherwood Anderson's "I'm a Fool," and Ring Lardner's "Some Like Them Cold," that story which seems to me as shrewd a picture of every woman at some time as is Chekhov's "The Darling." Now what do *you* like best?) The book also includes "Fifty Grand," "In Another Country," and the delicate and tragic "Hills Like White Elephants." I do not know where a greater collection of stories can be found.

Ford Madox Ford has said of this author, "Hemingway writes like an angel." I take issue (there is nothing better for that morning headache than taking a little issue). Hemingway writes like a human being. I think it is impossible for him to write of any event at which he has not been present; his is, then, a reportorial talent, just as Sinclair Lewis's is. But, or so I think, Lewis remains a reporter and Hemingway stands a genius because Hemingway has an unerring sense of selection. He discards details with a magnificent lavishness; he keeps his words to their short path. His is, as any reader knows, a dangerous influence. The simple thing he does looks so easy to do. But look at the boys who try to do it.

October 29, 1927

¶ Bruce Barton (1886–1967), of the famous Madison Avenue advertising establishment, wrote a life of Jesus called *The Man Nobody Knows*. . . . Mary Roberts Rinehart (1876–1958) was known for her mystery stories and as a popular society novelist.

The Professor Goes In for Sweetness and Light

¶ Professor William Lyon Phelps, presumably for God, for Country and for Yale, has composed a work on happiness. He calls it, in a word, *Happiness,* and he covers the subject in a volume about six inches tall, perhaps four inches across, and something less than half an inch thick. There is something rather magnificent in disposing, in an opus the size of a Christmas card, of this thing that men since time started have been seeking, pondering, struggling for, and guessing at. It reminds me, though the sequence may seem a bit hazy, of a time that I was lunching at the Cap d'Antibes (oh, I get around). I remarked, for I have never set up any claim to being a snappy luncheon companion, that somewhere ahead of us in the Mediterranean lay the island where the Man in the Iron Mask had been imprisoned.

"And who," asked my neighbor at the table, "was the Man in the Iron Mask?"

My only answer was a prettily crossed right to the jaw. How expect one who had had a nasty time of it getting through grammar school to explain to him, while he finished the rest of his filet, an identity that the big boys had never succeeded in satisfactorily working out, though they gave their years to the puzzle?

Somewhere, there, is an analogy, in a small way, if you have the patience for it. But I guess it isn't a very good anecdote. I'm better at animal stories.

Anyway, there is this to be said for a volume such as Professor Phelps's *Happiness*. It is second only to a rubber duck as the ideal bathtub companion. It may be held in the hand without causing muscular fatigue or nerve strain, it may be neatly balanced back of the faucets, and it may be read through before the water has cooled. And if it slips down the drain pipe, all right, it slips down the drain pipe.

The professor starts right off with "No matter what may be one's nationality, sex, age, philosophy, or religion, everyone wishes either to become or to remain happy." Well, there's no arguing that one. The author has us there. There is the place for getting out the pencil, underscoring the lines, and setting "how true," followed by several carefully executed exclamation points, in the margin. It is regrettable that the book did not come out during the season when white violets were in bloom, for there is the very spot to press one.

"Hence," goes on the professor, "definitions of happiness are interesting." I suppose the best thing to do with that is to let it pass. Me, I never saw a definition of happiness that could detain me after train-time, but that may be a matter of lack of opportunity, of inattention, or of congenital rough luck. If definitions of happiness can keep

Professor Phelps on his toes, that is little short of dandy. We might just as well get on along to the next statement, which goes like this: "One of the best" (we are still on definitions of happiness) "was given in my Senior year at college by Professor Timothy Dwight: 'The happiest person is the person who thinks the most interesting thoughts.'" Promptly one starts recalling such Happiness Boys as Nietzsche, Socrates, de Maupassant, Jean-Jacques Rousseau, William Blake, and Poe. One wonders, with hungry curiosity, what were some of the other definitions that Professor Phelps chucked aside in order to give preference to this one.

Here is a book happily free from iconoclasm. There is not a sentence that you couldn't read to your most conservative relatives and still be reasonably sure of that legacy. If you like—and please do—there might be here set down a few of the professor's conclusions. "Money is not the chief factor in happiness." . . . "Leave out the things that injure, cultivate the things that strengthen, and good results follow." . . . "I am certain that with the correct philosophy it is possible to have within one's possession sources of happiness that cannot permanently be destroyed." . . . "We are in a certain sense forced to lead a lonely life, because we have all the days of our existence to live with ourselves." . . . "Many go to destruction by the alcoholic route because they cannot endure themselves." . . . "Happiness is not altogether a matter of luck. It is dependent on certain conditions." These are but a few. But I give you my word, in the entire book there is nothing that cannot be said aloud in mixed company. And there is, also, nothing that makes you a bit the wiser. I wonder—oh, what will you think of me—if those two statements do not verge upon the synonymous.

Happiness concludes with a pretty tribute to what the professor calls the American cow. The cow, he points out, does not have to brush her teeth, bob her hair, select garments, light her fire and cook her food. She is not passionate about the income tax or the League of Nations; she has none of the thoughts that inflict distress and torture. "I have observed many cows," says the professor, in an interesting glimpse of autobiography, "and there is in their beautiful eyes no perplexity; their serene faces betray no apprehension or alarm; they are never even bored." He paints a picture of so sweet, so placid, so carefree an existence, that you could curse your parents for not being Holsteins. And then what does he do? Breaks up the whole lovely thing by saying, "Very few human beings would be willing to change into cows. . . . Life, with all its sorrows, perplexities, and heartbreaks, is more interesting than bovine placidity, hence more desirable. The more interesting it is, the happier it is." (Oh, professor, I should like to contest that.) "And the happiest person is the person who thinks the most interesting thoughts."

These are the views, this is the dogma, of Professor William Lyon Phelps, the pride of New Haven. And, of course, at Harvard there is now—and it looks as if there might be always—President Lowell, of the Fuller Committee. I trust that my ¶

son will elect to attend one of the smaller insti-
tutions of higher education.

November 5, 1927

¶ WILLIAM LYON PHELPS (1865–1943), in addition to
teaching at Yale, lectured widely on books to women's-club
audiences and was regarded by many in the twenties and
thirties as the arbiter of popular reading taste. . . . ABBOTT
LAWRENCE LOWELL (1856–1943), President of Harvard,
served on the Commission appointed by Governor Fuller of
Massachusetts, after the public clamor against the murder
conviction of radicals Sacco and Vanzetti in 1921, to
investigate the fairness of the trial. The Commission's finding
in favor of the court was widely unpopular with liberals.
Dorothy Parker joined the protest demonstrations in Boston
and was arrested and fined five dollars. Sacco and Vanzetti
were executed on October 22, 1927—a few days before this
issue of *The New Yorker* went to press.

Madame Glyn
Lectures on "It,"
with Illustrations

And this, ladies and gentlemen, is the finest day that has yet broken over the bloody and bowed head of your girl-friend. On this day there first fell into these trembling hands The Book, the Ultimate Book. There is grave doubt that I shall ever be able to talk of anything else. Certainly, I have read my last word. Print can hold for me now nothing but anticlimaxes. *It,* the chef d'oeuvre of Madame Elinor Glyn, has come into my life. And Sherman's coming into Atlanta is but a sneaking, tiptoe performance in comparison.

I didn't know. Truly, I didn't know. Mine is a life sheltered to the point of stuffiness. I attend no movies, for any motion-picture theatre is as an enlarged and a magnificently decorated lethal chamber to me. I have read but little of Madame Glyn. I did not know that things like "It" were going on. I have misspent my days. When I think of all those hours I flung away in reading William James and Santayana, when I might have been reading of life, throbbing, beating, perfumed life, I practically break down. Where, I ask you, have I been, that no true word of Madame Glyn's literary feats has come to me?

But even those far, far better informed than I must work a bit over the opening sentence of

Madame Glyn's foreword to her novel. "This is *not*," she says, drawing her emeralds warmly about her, "the story of the moving picture entitled, *It*, but a full character study of the story *It*, which the people in the picture read and discuss." I could go mad, in a nice way, straining to figure that out. But I shall let it stay a mystery. I shall take what comes to me, glad and grateful and unquestioning. After all, what more could one ask than a character study of a story?

Also in her foreword, Madame Glyn goes into the real meaning of "It." "To have 'It,'" she says—and is she the girl that knows?—"the fortunate possessor must have that strange magnetism which attracts both sexes." (Pul-ease, Madame Glyn, pul-ease!) "He or she must be entirely unself-conscious and full of self-confidence, indifferent to the effect he or she is producing, and uninfluenced by others." (Why, it's Levine, that's who it is, it's Levine.) "There must be physical attraction, but beauty is unnecessary. Conceit or self-consciousness destroys 'It' immediately. In the animal world, 'It' demonstrates" (*sic. Sic* as a dog.) "in tigers and cats—both animals being fascinating and mysterious and quite unbiddable."

So there you have it, in a coconut-shell. Now we can go on with the story.

Well, it seems there was this man named John Gaunt. By the time we meet him, there is iron-gray in his hair and he has twenty million dollars to go with it, but things were not always thus with him. At the age of ten, he was selling papers on the Bowery; yet he pulled himself up so sturdily that at forty he "was a person of great cultivation." Also, "he had that nameless charm, with a strong magnetism that can only be called 'It,' and cats, as well as women, always knew when he came into a room." Also, "from his fifteenth year, when the saloonkeeper's wife at the corner of his street groveled before his six feet of magnificent stripling strength, to his fortieth birthday, females of all types and classes manifested ardent passion for him." That, my friends, is living.

Then there was this girl, Ava Cleveland, and her brother Larry. Larry had It something terrible, and he also had a little way of taking opium. (Oh, please wait a minute. I think I'm going to be able to use "opium" in a sentence. I opium mother is feeling better. No, I guess I'm not, either.) Ava was young and slender and proud. And she had It. It, hell; she had Those.

But Ava was worried. There was that big bill at the dressmaker's. And she had been unlucky at baccarat, lately. And she and Larry were but hangers-on of the rich. You see, as one of Madame Glyn's characters explains, "Their father never brought them up to do anything, and then died." Died happy, you gather from this succinct biography, in the knowledge of a task accomplished, and nothing more to do.

So Ava was worried. Indeed, at the end of the very first chapter, we get a sharp flash of her terrible state of mind. " 'What the H—— are we to do?' she said to herself in not very polite English." Madame Glyn, as you see, does not flinch from plain talk. When she presents a street-Arab to us she has him cry, "Well, I'll be d——d!" It looks to me as if, out in Hollywood, she must have been on the adjoining lot to that on which *What Price Glory?* was being filmed.

Well, anyway, Ava was worried. Oh, of course there were things she could have done. But she was one who could not Give All unless she loved. Call it her hard luck, if you will, but that's how she was. She was unapproachable, pure, sacred. She could have made any All-American team in a moment, just on her dexterity at intercepting passes. Take her, for example, when the husband of her friend pleads with her—when he says:

" 'Then my moment will come—you can't do me down forever, child—I love your white skin.'

"A fierce gleam now came into Ava's eyes.

" 'You make me sick—you married men—it is nothing but skin—skin!' "

She did have a rich suitor, and of honorable intent, but he had a mother fixation that belonged by rights in the Smithsonian Institution. Thus did she put him in his place:

" 'I think a man is no man unless the woman he loves—the prospective mother of his children, who will carry on his name—stands above everything in his life—everything except his duty to his country and his own soil! ' "

But strong as is the temptation to quote and quote and quote, we must get on with the story. We must respect Madame Glyn's duty to her own soil. Well, it turns out that Ava and John meet, and he begins promptly to "vibrate with passion." But she is too proud to be mastered by one not of her class; indeed, to herself she refers to him as "this parvenue," with a convincingly aristocratic disregard for gender. And John Gaunt is one of those boys that must master his woman. Madame Glyn, in fact, has interestingly entangled his It with sadism all through the book, and maybe there is much to be said on her side. John must humble this disdainful creature; he must draw the net close.

So he gives Larry, the poppy-fancier, a job in his San Francisco office, and who would like to bet, then and there, that Larry isn't going to misappropriate funds? Then, when Ava's worries bring her to it, she seeks a position in his New York office, where he may keep his burning green eyes on her—I give you my word, she can feel them blazing through the massive oak door. She is offered a hundred dollars a week for cutting clippings out of newspapers. P.S. She got the job.

It goes on for nearly three hundred pages, with both of them vibrating away like steam launches. And then Larry comes through and steals two thousand dollars. Ava must have the money to keep Larry out of jail, where he couldn't get his hop. She goes to John's palatial residence. She will do it. She will Go Through. She will Sell Herself.

And then what do you think? She finds out it isn't the money; it isn't the principle of the thing, either. It is because she Loves. And what else do you think? He was going to marry her all the time.

Do you wonder that I am never going to read anything else?

November 26, 1927

¶ ELINOR GLYN (1864–1943), English author of sultry romances, is characterized by a popular jingle of the time: "Would you like to sin/With Elinor Glyn/On a tiger skin/ Or would you prefer/To err with her/On some other fur?"

The Socialist Looks
at Literature

¶ Upton Sinclair is his own King Charles' head. He cannot keep himself out of his writings, try though he may; or, by this time, try though he doesn't. Let him start off upon an essay on a subject miles away from his own concerns, and in half a minute there he'll be, popping up between the sentences with a tale of some old but still throbbing grievance, or of some recent wrong that has been worked upon him. His *Money Writes!* is far less the collected accusations against American authors that, according to rumor, he intended it to be than it is a running record of personal woes. As such, it is an interesting document, but one a little less than convincing. As the book goes on, you have your choice of two impressions of its author, as he is today: either he is the prey of delusions of persecution—and the man, God knows, has been beset so sorely and so thoroughly that fantasies of a vast conspiracy against him were almost inevitable; or else he has become a confirmed belly-acher. Many Socialists, and I say it though my heart and soul are with the cause of Socialism, get to be that way.

To me, Upton Sinclair is one of the American great. I have no words worthy of being laid before his courage, his passion, his integrity. Also I think, and I choose my phrase with precision, that he is a hell of a good writer. In Russia and the Scandinavian countries, I am told—me, I could number my Russian and Scandinavian acquaintances on the thumbs of my two hands—he is rated first among American authors, and those boys in the cold lands are no fools about literature. It seems to me that he has good reason to be hurt at the scant critical appreciation he receives in the United States; although I do not believe, as he does, that this indifference is due to the machinations of Wall Street. I think he is a fine novelist. And I think as a literary critic he is simply god-awful.

Of *Money Writes!*—I hate that exclamation point—he says in his foreword, "it is not a polite book, but it is an honest book, and it is needed." "Needed by whom?" one can only murmur, on finishing it. "This book," he says, further, "is a study of American literature from an economic point of view. It takes our living writers, and turns their pockets inside out, asking 'Where did you get it?' and 'What did you do for it?' "

Fired by Mr. Sinclair's example, I tried turning inside out the pockets of a living writer of my acquaintance, a writer considered successful in his work, and one who appears often in the wealthier magazines. The gross receipts were one nail file; one rubberized tobacco pouch; one fountain pen without a top; one Western Union envelope (empty); one folded bit of paper upon which was written "Endicott 6281—about eleven o'clock"; one card bearing the names Tony, Gus, and Joe, and a West Forty-eighth Street address;

one small rubber band (broken); one office clip (bent S-shaped); one half-dollar, one dime, and four pennies; one twenty-five-centimes piece; and several unpleasantly mouselike formations of gray fluff. I had no heart to ask, "Where did you get it?" much less, "What did you do for it?"

But Mr. Sinclair was luckier. He asked his questions and then supplied his own answers to them. And he did not confine himself, despite his promise in the preface, to turning inside out the pockets of the living. The book contains a piece on Amy Lowell in which he asserts that she was regarded as a poet only because she was of the Boston Lowells (oh, yes, yes, yes, of course he refers to her as a Brahmin) and had a house in Brookline where she entertained those editors whose pages she wished to use. "She had a huge mansion to live in," he says, "full of all the old books, and her mill-slaves enabled her to buy the new ones. . . . Her success is one more demonstration of the fact that if you have money and social prestige you can get away with murder in America." All right, Mr. Sinclair. What about young Cornelius Vanderbilt, for instance?

There is also his essay on George Sterling, which as a piece of good taste ranks with that statuette of the Milo Venus with the clock in her stomach. The poet had loved the woman who is now Upton Sinclair's wife; and Upton Sinclair writes of that deep and agonized love with a curious satisfaction, with a swagger, almost a smirk. He cannot limit his references to it to this one essay; he keeps dragging it in, though he must go and fetch it from afar, all through the book. I know that an author must be brave enough to chop away clinging tentacles of good taste for the sake of a great work. But this is no great work, you see.

Despite his persecutions, Mr. Sinclair reveals himself in *Money Writes!* to be an enviable man. Always the thing he desires to believe is the thing he feels he knows to be true. Regarding American literature, he is not hurt, but terribly, terribly angry. Well, many feel that way, but Mr. Sinclair's is a more specialized soreness. He is off American authors because they do not always write of sweat-shops and child-labor, of mill-slaves and strikes and wages. Let them write of anything else, and he says that their purses are fat, their livers white, and their tongues black with boot-polish. And he says it so loud and so hard that it sounds to him like truth.

Surely there is no denying that a great novel of social conditions would be a boon to American letters. But it does seem to be not especially useful to roar and stamp because certain authors choose to speak of jade and satin and the shining surface of old furniture. There is a certain lack of proportion in bringing heavy artillery to bear on Joseph Hergesheimer for so innocuous a work as *From an Old House*. Mr. Sinclair quotes from that book: "The bed in the curly maple room had a canopy like a film, a suspended tracery of frost; and under it many delicate and beautiful women had slept . . . cooled in the white silence of winter." Immediately he resumes his own words: "And against that lovely sentence" (Mr. Sinclair is never at his happiest in irony) "let us set one from an article in the *Survey*, December 15, 1925, by Dr. I. M. Rubinow, director of the Jewish Welfare Society of Philadelphia: 'The workingman's apartment in Philadelphia is not an apartment at all, but only two or three rooms sublet without any necessary adjustment for a separate decent family existence, for it has no private bathing or toilet facilities, and very frequently no separate water supply.' "

If this, ladies and gentlemen, proves anything at all, I am the Seventh Regiment. And if it is literary criticism, I am the National Guard.

As to the American poets, Mr. Sinclair shudders at the thought of those filthy traitors who write of love and death instead of sweat and oil. Yet his own knowledge of poetry seems to be a shade inadequate. I do not mean that only a Keats may write of poetry, but when Mr. Sinclair deems a certain verse of his own worthy of quoting—well, you'll see what I mean in a minute. It is a burlesque of the famous land-of-the-bean-and-the-cod lines, and it goes like this:

> Here's to the city of Boston,
>   The land of the bean and the cod,
> Where the Lowells won't let you buy *Oil!*
>   And you send to New York, by God.

December 10, 1927

¶ Although Upton Sinclair (1878–1968) was already famous for his social-protest novels such as *The Jungle*, about the Chicago meat-packing industry, and *Oil!*, which was banned in Boston, his eleven popular Lanny Budd novels were more than a decade in the future. . . . Joseph Hergesheimer (1880–1954), popular novelist of some literary distinction, was best known for his *Java Head*.

The Short Story, through a Couple of the Ages

There was a time, when I still had my strength, that I read nearly all the stories in the more popular magazines. I did not have to do it; I did it for fun, for I had yet to discover that there were other and more absorbing diversions that had the advantage of being no strain on the eyes. But even in those days of my vigor, nearly all the stories was the best that I could do. I could never go the full course. From the time I learned to read—which, I am pretty thoroughly convinced, was when I made my first big mistake—I was always unable to do anything whatever with stories that began in any of these following manners:

(1) "Ho, Felipe, my horse, and *pronto!*" cried *El Sol*. He turned to the quivering girl, and his mocking bow was so low that his *sombrero* swept the flags of the *patio*. "*Adiós,* then, *señorita,* until *mañana!*" And with a flash of white teeth across the lean young swarthiness of his face, he bounded to the back of his horse and was off, swift as a homing *paloma*.

(2) Everybody in Our Village loved to go by Granny Wilkins' cottage. Maybe it was the lilacs that twinkled a cheery greeting in the dooryard, or maybe it was the brass knocker that twinkled

on the white-painted door, or maybe—and I suspect this was the real reason—it was Granny herself, with her crisp white cap, and her wise brown eyes, twinkling away in her dear little old winter apple of a face.

(3) The train chugged off down the long stretch of track, leaving the little new schoolmistress standing alone on the rickety boards that composed the platform of Medicine Bend station. She looked very small indeed, standing there, and really ridiculously young. "I just won't cry!" she said fiercely, swallowing hard. "I won't! Daddy—Daddy would be disappointed in me if I cried. Oh, Daddy—Daddy, I miss you so!"

(4) The country club was ahum, for the final match of the Fourth of July Golf Tournament was in full swing. Many a curious eye lingered on Janet DeLancey, rocking lazily, surrounded as usual by a circle of white-flanneled adorers, for the porch was a-whisper with the rumor that the winner of the match would also be the winner of the hitherto untouched heart of the blond and devastating Janet.

(5) I dunno ez I ought to be settin' here, talkin', when there's the vittles to git fer the men-folks. But, Laws, 'tain't often a body hez a chanct ter talk, up this-a-way. I wuz tellin' yuh 'bout li'l Mezzie Meigs, ol' Skin-flint Meigs's da'ter. She wuz a right peart 'un, Mezzie wuz, and purty!

(6) "For God's sake, don't do it, Kid!" whispered Annie the Wop, twining her slim arms about the Kid's bull-like neck. "Yer promised me yer'd go straight, after the last time. The bulls'll get yer, Kid; they'll send yer up, sure. Aw, Kid, put away yer gat, and let's beat it away somewhere

in God's nice, clean country, where yer can raise chickens, like yer always dreamed of doin'."

But, with these half-dozen exceptions, I read all the other short stories that separated the Ivory Soap advertisements from the pages devoted to Campbell's Soups. I read about bored and pampered wives who were right on the verge of eloping with slender-fingered, quizzical-eyed artists, but did not. I read of young suburban couples, caught up in the fast set about them, driven to separation by their false, nervous life, and restored to each other by the opportune illness of their baby. I read tales proving that Polack servant-girls have their feelings, too. I read of young men who collected blue jade, and solved mysterious murders, on the side. I read stories of transplanted Russians, of backstage life, of shop-girls' evening hours, of unwanted grandmothers, of heroic collies, of experiments in child-training, of golden-hearted cow-punchers with slow drawls, of the comicalities of adolescent love, of Cape Cod fisherfolk, of Creole belles and beaux, of Greenwich Village, of Michigan Boulevard, of the hard-drinking and easy-kissing younger generation, of baseball players, sideshow artists, and professional mediums. I read, in short, more damn tripe than you ever saw in your life.

And then I found that I was sluggish upon awakening in the morning, spots appeared before my eyes, and my friends shunned me. I also found that I was reading the same stories over and over, month after month. So I stopped, like that. It is only an old wives' tale that you have to taper off.

Recently, though, I took the thing up again. There were rumors about that the American short story had taken a decided turn for the better. Crazed with hope, I got all the more popular and less expensive magazines that I could carry on my shoulders, and sat down for a regular old read. And a regular old read is just what it turned out to be. There they all were—the golden-hearted cow-punchers, the suburban couples, the baseball players, the Creole belles—even dear old Granny Wilkins was twinkling away, in one of them. There were the same old plots, the same old characters, the same old phrases—dear Heaven, even the same old illustrations. So that is why I shot myself.

It is true that in the magazines with quieter covers, with smaller circulations, and with higher purchasing prices, there are good short stories. Their scholarly editors have extended a courteous welcome to the newer writers. And the newer writers are good; they write with feeling and honesty and courage, and they write well. They do not prostitute their talents for money; they do not add words because they are to be paid by the word; scarcely, indeed, do they violate their amateur standing. But here, just as one did in the old days, does one get the feeling of reading the same stories over and over, month after month. There are no golden-hearted cow-punchers, but there are the inevitable mid-western farm families; the laughing Creole belles have given place to the raw tragedies of the Bayou; but the formulae are as rigorous. You must write your story as starkly as it was written just before you did it; if you can out-stark the previous author, you are one up. Sedulous agony has become as monotonous as sedulous sunshine. Save for those occasions when you come upon a Hemingway or an Anderson or a Lardner in your reading, the other stories that meet your eye might all have come from the same pen.

I do not see how Mr. Edward O'Brien stands the strain. Season after season, as inescapable as Christmas, he turns out his collection of what he considers to be the best short stories of their year. To do this, and he does it conscientiously, he must read and rate every short story in every American magazine of fiction. Me, I should liefer adopt the career of a blood donor.

The Best Short Stories of 1927 is distinguished by the inclusion in it of Ernest Hemingway's superb "The Killers." This is enough to make any book of stories a notable one. There is also Sherwood Anderson's "Another Wife," which seems to me one of his best. But in the other stories I can find only disappointment. They seem to me wholly conventional, in this recent convention-ality of anguish. There is no excitement to them; they have all the dogged quiet of too-careful writ-ing. Separate, each one might possibly—oh, pos-sibly—grip you. Grouped together, they string out as flat as Kansas.

Their compiler shows himself, in this volume, to be more than ever the unsung hero. In the back of the book, where he lists all the short stories of the year, and grades them, unasked, without a star, with one star, with two stars, or with three stars, according to his notion of their merits, you may gain some idea of what the man has been through. I give you some of the titles of the stories that he has wrestled with:

"Vomen Is Easily Veak-Minded"; "Ma Bent-

ley's Christmas Dinner"; "Archibald in Arcady"
(there is always one of those, every year); "Fred
and Circuses"; "Willie Painter Stays on the Lev-
vel"; "Sylvia Treads among the Goulds"; "Betty
Use Your Bean"; "Daddy's Nondetachable Cuffs";
"Ann 'n' Andy"; "Freed 'Em and Weep" (I bet
that was a little love); "Jerry Gums the Game";
"Blue Eyes in Trouble"; "Grandflapper" (you
can practically write that one for yourself); "She
Loops to Conquer"; "Yes, Sir, He's My Maybe";
and "Dot and Will Find Out What It Means to
Be Rich," which last sets me wondering into the
night just what were the titles that the author
threw out as being less adroit.

They say Mr. O'Brien makes ample money, on
his sales of these stories written by others, and I
hope it is true. But no matter how much it is, he
deserves more.

December 17, 1927

Mrs. Post Enlarges on Etiquette

Emily Post's *Etiquette* is out again, this time in a new and an enlarged edition, and so the question of what to do with my evenings has been all fixed up for me. There will be an empty chair at the deal table at Tony's, when the youngsters gather to discuss life, sex, literature, the drama, what is a gentleman, and whether or not to go on to Helen Morgan's Club when the place closes; for I shall be at home among my book. I am going in for a course of study at the knee of Mrs. Post. Maybe, some time in the misty future, I shall be Asked Out, and I shall be ready. You won't catch me being intentionally haughty to subordinates or refusing to be a pallbearer for any reason except serious ill health. I shall live down the old days, and with the help of Mrs. Post and God (always mention a lady's name first) there will come a time when you will be perfectly safe in inviting me to your house, which should never be called a residence except in printing or engraving.

It will not be a grueling study, for the sprightliness of Mrs. Post's style makes the textbook as fascinating as it is instructive. Her characters, introduced for the sake of example, are called by no such unimaginative titles as Mrs. A., or Miss Z., or Mr. X.; they are Mrs. Worldly, Mr. Bachelor, the Gildings, Mrs. Oldname, Mrs. Neighbor, Mrs. Stranger, Mrs. Kindhart, and Mr. and Mrs. Nono Better. This gives the work all the force and the application of a morality play.

It is true that occasionally the author's invention plucks at the coverlet, and she can do no better by her brain-children than to name them Mr. Jones and Mrs. Smith. But it must be said, in fairness, that the Joneses and the Smiths are the horrible examples, the confirmed pullers of social boners. They deserve no more. They go about saying "Shake hands with Mr. Smith" or "I want to make you acquainted with Mrs. Smith" or "Will you permit me to recall myself to you?" or "Pardon *me!*" or "Permit me to assist you" or even "Pleased to meet you!" One pictures them as small people, darting about the outskirts of parties, fetching plates of salad and glasses of punch, applauding a little too enthusiastically at the end of a song, laughing a little too long at the point of an anecdote. If you could allow yourself any sympathy for such white trash, you might find something pathetic in their eagerness to please, their desperate readiness to be friendly. But one must, after all, draw that line somewhere, and Mr. Jones, no matter how expensively he is dressed, always gives the effect of being in his shirt-sleeves, while Mrs. Smith is so unmistakably the daughter of a hundred Elks. Let them be dismissed by somebody's phrase (I wish to heaven it were mine) —"the sort of people who buy their silver."

These people in Mrs. Post's book live and breathe; as Heywood Broun once said of the characters in a play, "they have souls and elbows."

Take Mrs. Worldly, for instance, Mrs. Post's heroine. The woman will live in American letters. I know of no character in the literature of the last quarter-century who is such a complete pain in the neck.

See her at that moment when a younger woman seeks to introduce herself. Says the young woman: " 'Aren't you Mrs. Worldly?' Mrs. Worldly, with rather freezing politeness, says 'Yes,' and waits." And the young woman, who is evidently a glutton for punishment, neither lets her wait from then on nor replies, "Well, Mrs. Worldly, and how would you like a good sock in the nose, you old meat-axe?" Instead she flounders along with some cock-and-bull story about being a sister of Millicent Manners, at which Mrs. Worldly says, "I want very much to hear you sing some time," which marks her peak of enthusiasm throughout the entire book.

See Mrs. Worldly, too, in her intimate moments at home. "Mrs. Worldly seemingly pays no attention, but nothing escapes her. She can walk through a room without appearing to look either to the right or left, yet if the slightest detail is amiss, an ornament out of place, or there is one dull button on a footman's livery, her house telephone is rung at once!" Or watch her on that awful night when she attends the dinner where everything goes wrong. "In removing the plates, Delia, the assistant, takes them up by piling one on top of the other, clashing them together as she does so. You can feel Mrs. Worldly looking with almost hypnotized fascination—as her attention might be drawn to a street accident against her will."

E

There is also the practical-joker side to Mrs. W. Thus does Mrs. Post tell us about that: "For example, Mrs. Worldly writes:

" 'Dear Mrs. Neighbor:

" 'Will you and your husband dine with us very informally on Tuesday, the tenth, etc.'

"Whereupon, the Neighbors arrive, he in a dinner coat, she in her simplest evening dress, and find a dinner of fourteen people and every detail as formal as it is possible to make it. . . . In certain houses—such as the Worldlys' for instance—formality is inevitable, no matter how informal may be her 'will you dine informally' intention."

One of Mrs. Post's minor characters, a certain young Struthers, also stands sharply out of her pages. She has caught him perfectly in that scene which she entitles "Informal Visiting Often Arranged by Telephone" (and a darn good name for it, too). We find him at the moment when he is calling up Millicent Gilding, and saying, " 'Are you going to be in this afternoon?' She says, 'Yes, but not until a quarter of six.' He says, 'Fine, I'll come then.' Or she says, 'I'm so sorry, I'm playing bridge with Pauline—but I'll be in tomorrow!' He says, 'All right, I'll come tomorrow.' " Who, ah, who among us does not know a young Struthers?

As one delves deeper and deeper into *Etiquette*, disquieting thoughts come. That old Is-It-Worth-It Blues starts up again, softly, perhaps, but plainly. Those who have mastered etiquette, who are entirely, impeccably right, would seem to arrive at a point of exquisite dullness. The letters and the conversations of the correct, as quoted by Mrs. Post, seem scarcely worth the striving for. The rules for the finding of topics of conversation fall damply on the spirit. "You talk of something you have been doing or thinking about—planting a garden, planning a journey, contemplating a journey, or similar safe topics. Not at all a bad plan is to ask advice: "We want to motor through the South. Do you know about the roads?' Or, 'I'm thinking of buying a radio. Which make do you think is best?' "

I may not dispute Mrs. Post. If she says that is the way you should talk, then, indubitably, that is the way you should talk. But though it be at the cost of that future social success I am counting on, there is no force great enough ever to make me say, "I'm thinking of buying a radio."

It is restful, always, in a book of many rules—and *Etiquette* has six hundred and eighty-four pages of things you must and mustn't do—to find something that can never touch you, some law that will never affect your ways. . . .

And in *Etiquette*, too, I had the sweetly restful moment of chancing on a law which I need not bother to memorize, let come no matter what. It is in that section called "The Retort Courteous to One You Have Forgotten," although it took a deal of dragging to get it in under that head. "If," it runs, "after being introduced to you, Mr. Jones" (of course, it would be Mr. Jones that would do it) "calls you by a wrong name, you let it pass, at first, but if he persists you may say: 'If you please, my name is Stimson.' "

No, Mrs. Post; persistent though Mr. Smith be, I may not say, "If you please, my name is Stimson." The most a lady may do is give him the wrong telephone number.

December 31, 1927

Poor, Immortal Isadora

My Life, the posthumously published autobiography of Isadora Duncan, is to me an enormously interesting and a profoundly moving book. Here was a great woman; a magnificent, generous, gallant, reckless, fated fool of a woman. There was never a place for her in the ranks of the terrible, slow army of the cautious. She ran ahead, where there were no paths.

She was no writer, God knows. Her book is badly written, abominably written. There are passages of almost idiotic naïveté, and there are passages of horrendously flowery verbiage. There are veritable Hampton Court mazes of sentences. There are long, low moans of poetry, painstakingly interpolated. There are plural pronouns, airily relating to singular nouns. She knew all about herself as an author. She says, in her introduction, "It has taken me years of struggle, hard work and research to learn to make one simple gesture, and I know enough about the Art" (that word she always capitalizes) "of writing to realise that it would take me again just so many years of concentrated effort to write one simple, beautiful sentence." But, somehow, the style of the book makes no matter.

Out of this mess of prose come her hope, her passion, her suffering; above all, comes the glamour that was Isadora Duncan's.

"Glamour" and "glamorous" are easy words, these days. The, shall we say, critical writers scoop them up by the handsful and plaster the fences of the town with them. The, shall we also say, intelligentsia fling them about like coppers, for the urchins to dive for. The other day, I heard the term "glamorous" applied three times within minutes. It was bestowed upon (*a*) a pretty little actress correctly performing a suitable little part in a neat little play; (*b*) an expensively dressed, nervous woman in whose drawing-room one may meet over-eager portrait-painters, playwrights of dubious sexes, professional conversationalists, and society ladies not yet quite divorced; and (*c*) a graceful young man ever carefully dropping references to his long, unfinished list of easy conquests. Well, there are always those who cannot distinguish between glitter and glamour, just as there are always those who cannot understand why you should desire real pearls when they can't be told from the imitations. But you can, you see, tell them from the imitations. The neat surfaces of the imitations shine prettily; the real glow from within. And the glamour of Isadora Duncan came from her great, torn, bewildered, foolhardy soul.

This book takes her up only to her departure for Russia to found a school of dancing, in 1921; it does not tell of her fantastically ill-advised marriage, and of her few blurred, dizzy years thereafter. There was to be another volume, but she never started it.

A little while after this one had reached her

publishers, she was dead. She died as she should die, dramatically and without warning. It is curious that, almost on the first page of her book, she says, "I was born by the sea, and I have noticed that all the great events of my life have taken place by the sea." She died by the sea, on that shiny avenue of Nice that follows the Mediterranean. It is curious, too, that she died in an automobile accident, as did her two exquisite children. She never recovered from their deaths. Oh, she tried. You follow, in her ill-written pages, the way she tried to live again. She drank, and she loved, and she danced. But she never again became the Bacchante, the beloved, the high priestess of her Art. From the day they were killed until the day of her own death, she was Niobe.

I do not know how honest her book is. I am convinced that as she set down each event, she believed that she was representing it in absolute truth, for she was of the accursed race of artists, who believe each thing they say while they are saying it; yes, and who would go to the stake for that moment's belief. She speaks with frankness—though frankness, if you will forgive dogma, is no synonym for honesty—of her lovers. She had a knack for selecting the unworthy—perhaps all great women have; one and all, they treated her with an extraordinary shabbiness. She calls only one by name. The others, she refers to by gloriously romantic titles—"Romeo," or the "Archangel" (the Archangel, by the way, threw her flat for one of the little girls in her band of dancers), or "Lohengrin." "Lohengrin," whose true name we all know, was perhaps the most important fig-

ure in her life; certainly he was the most frequent.
He was generous to her only with money, and he
had so much of that that it was a tiny, an imper-
ceptible, form of generosity. But she never writes
of them ungallantly. She does not whine, nor seek
pity. She was a brave woman. We shall not look
upon her like again.

There is another heroine in her book, though
I doubt if the author realized it. That heroine is
her mother. Dora Duncan, a little, prim, conven-
tion-bound music-teacher, divorced her roving
husband. But she followed her children as anxiously and as loyally as a hen does a brood of
fluffy ducklings. Uncomplaining, she lived with
them in bare studios, where the only furniture,
the mattresses upon which they slept, was hidden
by day under Isadora's famous blue curtains. She
went with them to Greece, donned, with them,
tunic and chlamys and peplum—one hears her
saying, plaintively, "How does this thing go on?"
—and watched her son, Raymond, who always
was the boy to do the one thing too much, kneeling down and kissing the soil, to the reasonable
astonishment of the natives. She saw Isadora come
into fame and fortune; beheld the contracts, that
would have meant a secure old age for her, awaiting her daughter's signature; and then saw Isadora
tear them up because she was interested, at the
moment, in some transient young man. Finally,
she came back to America, to live the rest of her
days—you see, in the book you see only Isadora's
version, but you can guess what a magnificent
battle it must have been—wanting no more to do
with any of her offspring. Isadora says that the
elderly crabbedness, and the desertion, of her

mother was due to the fact that never, since her
husband left, had she taken a lover. But you can't
help feeling that this is not quite so. Mrs. Duncan
must have been so tired. Oh, so very tired.

Please read Isadora Duncan's *My Life.* You will
find you won't care how it is written; you will find
you will not be eager to trace to their sources the
current rumors that it has been expurgated. There
is enough in these pages. Here is the record of a
grand person. Undoubtedly she was trying. She
could not do anything that was not dramatic.
Take, for instance, the occasion of her cutting her
hair short. Other women go and have their hair
bobbed, and that is all there is to it. But Isadora—
she was in Albania with Raymond at the time—
writes, "I cut off my hair, and threw it in the
sea." She was like that. It comes, again, from be-
longing to that accursed race that cannot do anything unless they see, before and after, a tableau
of themselves in the deed.

Possibly I am unfair about the shabbiness of
her lovers. Surely there is much to be said on their
side. She must have been trying, with her constant
drama, with her intensity, with her pitiful, un-
dying hope that here was the love, the great,
beautiful love, that was to endure for all time.
But she gave them Excitement. She gave them
Glamour. She gave them a glimpse of Beauty.

> Fortunate they
> Who though once only, and then but far away
> Have heard her massive sandal set on stone.

They were lucky men, they were. But she was
not a lucky lady.

January 14, 1928

Re-enter Miss Hurst,
Followed by
Mr. Tarkington

It is with a deep, though a purely personal, regret that the conductor of this department announces the visitation upon her of a nasty case of the rams.

The rams, as I hope you need never find out for yourself, are much like the heebie-jeebies, except that they last longer, strike deeper, and are, in general, fancier. The illness was contracted on Thursday night at an informal gathering, and I am convinced it may be directly traced to the fact that I got a stalk of bad celery at dinner. It must have been bad celery; because you can't tell me that two or three sidecars, some champagne at dinner, and a procession of mixed Benedictines-and-brandies, taking seven hours to pass a given point, are going to leave a person in that state where she is afraid to turn around suddenly lest she see again a Little Mean Man about eighteen inches tall, wearing a yellow slicker and roller-skates. Besides the continued presence of the Little Mean Man, there are such minor symptoms as loss of correct knee action, heartbreak, an inability to remain either seated or standing, and a constant sound in the ears as of far-off temple bells. These, together with a readiness to weep at any minute and a racking horror of being left alone, positively identify the disease as the rams. Bad celery will give you the rams quicker than anything else. You want to look out for it. There's a lot of it around.

Additional proof that contaminated food was served to those attending Thursday night's *fiesta* is offered by a fellow guest—who, by the way, is also a contributor to this lucky magazine. Ever since the event, he has had the rams, and had them good. To the list of familiar lesser symptoms he adds an involuntary jittering movement of the hands, so pronounced as to render an ordinary teacup and saucer almost deafening in his clutch. He has not yet been followed about by any Little Mean Men on roller-skates; but, from the time of his awakening on Friday morning—an awakening which was entirely contrary to any wish of his— he has been attended by a personal beaver. He is all right so long as he keeps his eyes straight ahead. But if he forgets, and looks quickly up and to the left, he sees this beaver run like lightning across the ceiling. It is an unusually large beaver, he says, with the broadest, flattest tail he ever saw in his life. He says it looks to him to be a beaver of about four or five years of age.

He is assured that he owes his new pet to his having been the recipient, at Thursday night's social function, of a bad string bean. (The second quickest way to contract the rams is through bad string beans; you should always have your string beans analyzed.) So you can see for yourself what sort of food was provided for us. Criminal penny-pinching, that's what a thing like that is.

You can always tell if you have the genuine rams by the fact that you cannot like anything much, even your nearest and dearest. The milder form of the rams—called the German rams, or Jacob's Evil—attacks so lightly that it leaves you vitality enough occasionally to give a whoop about something. In the real, old-fashioned rams, there are two things that you desire to do less than all the things in the world. One is to read new books; and the other is to write about them. This latter activity is not only distasteful but downright dangerous. In the first place, it is practically impossible to keep the forehead off the typewriter keys. And in the second, the sufferer from the rams is very likely to contract a bad case of Author's Elbow, due to constant strenuous erasing of the curious designs made by his frequently hitting, in his weakened condition, several of the wrong letters and punctuation marks at once.

I give you these grim details only in apology. My tiny, begrudged enthusiasm and slow, reluctant words are not the results of a fit of the sulks, truly they are not. It must have been that bad celery that begot them. For I have read two novels that are selling by the thousands every day, and are, also daily, winning the plaudits of press and public. And for my life, I cannot discern what all the applause is about. That's what the rams do to a person.

A President Is Born—no, it is not a companion piece to the Nan Britton book, and if I never hear any such crack again, it will be too soon—is the latest Fannie Hurst novel. I have a deep admiration for Miss Hurst's work; possibly in your company I must admit this with a coo of deprecating laughter, as one confesses a fondness for comic strips, motion-picture magazines, chocolate-almond bars, and like too-popular entertainments. There have been times when her sedulously tortuous style, her one-word sentences and her curiously compounded adjectives, drive me into an irritation that is only to be relieved by kicking and screaming. But she sees and she feels, and she makes you see and feel; and those are not small powers. She has written nothing that has not, in some degree, moved me—nothing, at least, until she wrote *A President Is Born*.

This is, they say, her Big Novel. (If you were a real book reviewer, you would say, "Miss Hurst has chosen a far larger canvas than is her wont." I wish I could talk like that without getting all hot and red.) It is one of those things supposedly written from some time in the future—a trick which is to me, though I have no notion why, always vaguely annoying—and it relates the early life of one David Schuyler, a legendary and an heroic President of the United States. This early life occurs in the mid-western farmlands, and the boy is the youngest member of one of those mid-western farm families so numerous that you are constantly losing track of their names, dispositions, occupations, and spouses. There is among them one of those big, wise, calm, broad-hipped, level-eyed women who puts the farm on a paying basis by her efforts—why do our lady authors so love to write of those? This one, David's sister, is supposed to contribute the footnotes that, in their turn, are supposed to lend an air of authenticity to the book. Her manner of writing shows that she has been much influenced by Miss Hurst.

I can find in *A President Is Born* no character

nor any thought to touch or excite me. (There go those rams again.) I am awfully sorry, but it is to me a pretty dull book.

And I am sorry, too, about my feelings in regard to Booth Tarkington's new novel, *Claire Ambler*. It is, of course, written with finish and skill and a sense of leisured care. But its characters have extraordinarily few dimensions, even for Tarkington characters. It is the study of a girl, who wants to make men fall in love with her but doesn't want them to tell her about it, from the time she is eighteen until she reaches twenty-five. The first part of the book is perhaps the best, certainly the most amusing, for there Mr. Tarkington is dealing with adolescent love. And he has no equal at setting down in exquisite words the comic manifestations of youthful love-agony, though never does he dare let his pen touch the agony itself. He is, I am afraid, too merciful a man for greatness.

Claire Ambler was a disappointment to me, who have a naïve trust in what the critics say. I read it all; but I found that neither during the process nor after did I care very much.

There. Now you see what the rams can do. Please, oh, please, take warning, and be careful about celery and string beans.

January 28, 1928

¶ Fannie Hurst (1889–1968) was known at this time chiefly for her earlier novels *Humoresque* and *Lummox*. . . . Booth Tarkington (1869–1946) twice won the Pulitzer Prize for his novels, and his stories of adolescence, *Penrod* and *Seventeen,* were beloved by a whole generation.

A Good Novel,
and a Great Story

You don't want a general houseworker, do you?
Or a traveling companion, quiet, refined, speaks
fluent French entirely in the present tense? Or an
assistant billiard-maker? Or an elevator girl? Or
a magician's helper? Or a private librarian? Or
a lady car-washer? Because if you do, I should
appreciate your giving me a trial at the job. Any
minute, now, I am going to become one of the
Great Unemployed. I am about to leave literature
flat on its face. I don't want to review books any
more. It cuts in too much on my reading.

In order that my public—my boy and girl, I
call them—may have the inestimable benefit of
my report, I am supposed to have read *The Last
Post,* by Ford Madox Ford (*né* Hueffer). I have
been faithful to my duty, in my fashion. I have
read the book. But I did not behave like a regular
little soldier about it. I did not sit me down in a
hard, straight chair, and read it sternly through
at one stretch. I kept putting it down, and sneaking off to the dear, strange things I truly ached
to read and to ponder.

It is not that *The Last Post* is not a good book.
It is not that I do not think Ford Madox Ford is
a fine novelist. (There was a time, there, when I
thought I was never going to get out of those
negatives, but the crisis is passed, now, and I am

expected to pull through.) It is that there are certain things set down in black on white beside which even distinguished, searching, passionate novels pale to mediocrity.

There is, for example, a brief story lately printed in a morning paper. I cannot take my mind from that story. I read it over and over, and then I crawl off in a corner and think and think and think. If it were only any of my business, I should tell you about that story. It concerns a man who shall here be called William Doe, because he has enough trouble already. He was charged with writing what are journalistically called poison-pen letters to various city officials; the charge was dismissed when handwriting experts declared that the letters were written not by him but by a woman. That, I think, is a fairly good start, but wait. If it were any possible affair of mine, I should quote the cool, exact words of that newspaper story. "Look at this, will you?" I should say, and then I should write down these lines:

"Mr. Doe from the first stoutly denied that he had anything to do with the letters or knew anything about them. He was at a loss to explain them and the use of his name in the signatures. Yesterday he said that the only explanation he could think of was the fact that his mother had kept him and his brother in long dresses until they were nine years old and that he had since then frequently been a victim of practical jokes perpetrated by his childhood acquaintances."

The Last Post is a tale of human anguish, but it rings flat and thin compared with this short piece. "The Life of William Doe"—there would

be a book. I do not know who could worthily set
down this wretched, grinding tragedy, this tale of
small, steady tortures, of little obscene agonies
dropping, slowly, ceaselessly, upon the heart of a
man. Dreiser's pen is too heavy; Hemingway's,
too sharp. Lardner, I think, might do it. Sherwood Anderson—no, I guess not. But God send
that someone does it, and does it fittingly, for
there will be a great book—perhaps the great
book.

I wish I could stop thinking about it, for, as
you have so crisply remarked, it is none of my
damn business. I am here to write about books,
not to review newspaper stories. Who do I think
I am, anyway—Guy Fawkes?

Well, about this latest novel of Ford Madox
Ford's. It is the last of his series of four books—
what do you call a series of four books, anyway?
I can only count up to "trilogy"—beginning with
Some Do Not . . . and going on through *No
More Parades* and *A Man Could Stand Up*. To
me, *The Last Post* ranks fourth not only in sequence. Ford's style has here become so tortuous
that he writes almost as if he were parodying himself. There are grave hardships for the reader in
the long interior monologues which make up
much of the book. It is a novel to be read with a
furrow in the brow. You must constantly turn
back pages, to ascertain from inside which character's head the author is writing.

(What do you suppose were some of the other
dainty little practical jokes that William Doe's
childhood acquaintances played on him?)

Yet *The Last Post* is a novel worth all its diffi-
culties. There is always, for me, a vastly stirring

quality in Ford's work. His pages are quick and true. I know of few other novelists who can so surely capture human bewilderment and suffering, for his is a great pity. To me, his best book, and far and away his best, is *The Good Soldier*—the novel separate from the books about Christopher Tietjens. Yet all the books of the Tietjens saga have in them some of the same power, the same depth, the same rackingly moving honesty that makes *The Good Soldier* so high and fine a work. They are sad books, filled with sad and skinless people. There are some who do not like such books. The world, too, is crowded with the sorrowful and the sensitive. There are many who do not like such a world.

(Do you think that William Doe must trace every bitter thing that befalls him back to those first nine terrible years of his life? Do you think he has become obsessed with the thought? And if he has, why under Heaven shouldn't he have?)

In his dedicatory letter, which serves as a preface to *The Last Post*, Ford says that the book is written to satisfy a certain "stern, contemptuous, and almost virulent insistence on knowing 'what became of Tietjens.' " There was a demand for an ending; "if possible a happy ending." But that he was not able to supply. "For in this world of ours," he says, "though lives may end, Affairs do not. Even though Tietjens and Valentine were dead the Affair that they set going would go rolling on down the generations. . . . The rest will go on beneath the nut-boughs or over the seas—or in the best Clubs. It is not your day nor mine that shall see the end of them."

So at the end of this last book, Christopher

Tietjens, "The Last Tory," is left with Valentine and the child that is to be born to them, to carry on the Tietjens gentleness and courage and bewilderment. It has always been a thorn to me that the man should have so difficult a name as Christopher Tietjens; and as for the woman he loved, fine and brave though Ford has made her, I could never let her near my heart because her name was Valentine Wannop. That is quibbling, I know, and of the silliest sort. But that's the way I am. Take me or leave me; or, as is the usual order of things, both.

(I wonder if William Doe's brother, who was also condemned to those pitiful long dresses, has been a like victim of the hellish jokes of the childhood acquaintances. Or was it only William who was singled out?)

The Last Post is mainly the story of the life's end of Mark Tietjens, Christopher's brother, who neither spoke nor moved from the moment he heard a bugler blow the last post, the call for the dead, on the night of the Armistice that he thought shamed England and betrayed her sons, to the quarter-hour before his own death. Then he speaks one brief phrase of deep and contemptuous pity to Christopher's wife, the glamorous and devilish Sylvia. Sylvia, the villainess of the piece, is the character who stands out sharpest to me from the Tietjens saga. It is she that I am sorriest to see leave forever.

(Who do you suppose that woman was who wrote those atrocious letters and signed William Doe's name to them? She must be overwhelmed with the success of her prank. It was such a long, thorough, far-reaching bit of savagery. He was arrested in October, and knew three months of being out on a thousand dollars' bail.)

Through *The Last Post*, as through all his books, there run the long fibers of Ford's hatreds. That is all very well for a writer; that, in fact, is fine for a writer; but it may get him into messes. And it gets Ford into a nasty jam, when he comes to one of his characters, his Amurrican lady, Mrs. De Bray Pape. I am as ready as the next to take a joke on my native sex and my own country-women, but here is as clumsy a caricature as you can find. I suggest that Mr. Ford go some place and get good and ashamed of himself for smearing this blemish of heavy buffoonery across the honest pages of his book.

(I wonder if William Doe ever has easy moments. Or does he dwell always in the fear of what will happen next? Do you suppose he ever has any fun? And how does he?)

And now that this review is over, do you mind if I talk business for a moment? If you yourself haven't any spare jobs for a retired book-reviewer, maybe some friend of yours might have something. Maybe you wouldn't mind asking around. Salary is no object; I want only enough to keep body and soul apart. The one thing I ask is that I have an occasional bit of time to myself. I want to read the papers.

February 4, 1928

¶ FORD MADOX FORD (1873–1939) changed his surname from Hueffer during World War I. He later withdrew *The Last Post* from the *Parade's End* tetralogy, preferring to have the first three novels stand alone as a trilogy.

Literary Rotarians

The town, these days, is full of them. You cannot go ten yards, on any thoroughfare, without being passed by some Rotarian of Literature, hurrying to attend a luncheon, banquet, tea, or get-together, where he may rush about from buddy to buddy, slapping shoulders, crying nicknames, and swapping gossip of the writing game. I believed for as long as possible that they were on for their annual convention; and I thought that they must run their little span and disappear, like automobile shows, six-day bicycle races, ice on the pavements, and such recurrent impedimenta of metropolitan life. But it appears that they are to go on and on. Their fraternal activities are their livings—more, their existences. They are here, I fear, to stay. But they will never take the place of the horse.

The members of this benevolent order do not wear any such jolly paraphernalia as fezzes, plumed hats, animals' teeth, or fringed silk badges —or, at least, they have not yet done so. But you can spot any one of them at a glance. They are all bright and brisk and determinedly young. They skitter from place to place with a nervous quickness that suggests the movements of those little leggy things that you see on the surface of

ponds, on hot Summer days. The tips of their
noses are ever delicately a-quiver for the scent of
news, and their shining eyes are puckered a bit,
with the strain of constant peering. Their words
are quicker than the ear, and spoken always in
syncopation, from their habitually frantic haste
to get out the news that the Doran people have
tied up with the Doubleday, Page outfit, or that
McCall's Magazine has got a new high-pressure
editor. Some of them are women, some of them
are men. This would indicate that there will
probably always be more of them.

They have, I should judge, the best time of
any people in the world. Running from guild to
league to club to committee, and round the course
again, they meet only those of their kind, only
those who speak their language and share their
interests. They see no misunderstanding outsiders,
need listen to no tedious tales of struggle and
terror and injustice. Round and round they go,
ever up on their toes, giving and receiving hands
and smiles and cozily intimate words. It is all as
gay and active and wholesome as a figure in the
lancers.

Naturally, people so happy cannot keep all
their bliss bottled up inside themselves. It must
overflow somewhere; and it does, baby, it does.
Pick up a newspaper (it would be just like you
to pick up the *Wall Street Journal* and make a
fool out of me) and there, snug on an inside page,
you will find one of the jolly brotherhood bub-
bling away about the good times he and his bud-
dies have been having. These accounts are called
diaries or day-books or "Letters from a Penman"
or "Jottings on a Cuff" or "Helling Around with

the Booksy Folk" or—but no; there is one weekly
treat actually headed, "Turns with a Bookworm,"
so you can see how much use it is to try to kid
their titles. Anyway, it doesn't matter. All I
wanted to point out is that if a compositor, in
some moment of dreamy confusion, ran any such
column under the head of "Gleanings from
Rotary," he would still keep his job.

These reports are all written in the chatty, intimate manner; personality must be injected and
liveliness, so that you shall see that the writer,
for all his lofty connection with things literary,
can be just as good company as an electrician, say,
or a certified public accountant. And of what hot
doings do they tell! From noon to morning, theirs
is one mad whirl of literary gatherings. You read
and wonder, enviously, how they ever stand the
pace.

I went to a literary gathering once. How I got
there is all misty to me. I remember that, on that
afternoon, I was given a cup of tea which tasted
very strange. Drowsiness came over me, and there
was a humming noise in my ears; then everything
went black. When I came to my senses, I was in
the brilliantly lighted banquet-hall of one of the
large hotels, attending a dinner of a literary asso-
ciation. The place was filled with people who
looked as if they had been scraped out of drains.
The ladies ran to draped plush dresses—for Art;
to wreaths of silken flowerets in the hair—for
Femininity; and, somewhere between the two
adornments, to chain-drive *pince-nez*—for Astig-
matism. The gentlemen were small and somewhat in need of dusting. There were guests of
honor: a lady with three names, who composed

pageants; a haggard gentleman, who had won the prize of $20 offered by *Inertia: a Magazine of Poesy* for the best poem on the occupation of the Ruhr district; and another lady, who had completed a long work on "Southern Californian Bird-Calls" and was ready for play.

There was apparently some idea of seating the guests at various small oval tables, but the plan was not followed. Instead, there was incessant visiting, from table to table. No introductions were needed, for each guest wore a card with his or her name plainly written upon it, and everybody talked to everybody else. And the night hung still, to bear the weight of those words of who was cleaning up how much in the fiction game, or the poetry racket.

By pleading a return of that old black cholera of mine, I got away before the speeches, the songs, and the probable donning of paper caps and marching around the room in lockstep. I looked with deep interest, the next morning, for the bookmen's and bookwomen's accounts of the event. One and all, they declared that never had there been so glamorous and brilliant a function. You inferred that those who had been present would require at least a week to sleep it off. They wrote of it as they write of every other literary gathering—as if it were like one of those parties that used to occur just before Rome fell.

From that day to this, I have never touched another cup of tea.

Never has any member of literary Rotary been known to have a dull time. He meets no writer but to love him, no publisher but to praise. (Or however it goes, please.) He has yet to have a thin evening. He no more knows the meaning of the word "boredom" than he does that of the word "taste."

It is not only the altruism of effervescence that causes these scribes to share their gaieties with the public. There is prestige to be had from these accounts. To have written anything, whether it be a *Ulysses* or whether it be a report of who sat next to whom at the P.E.N. Club dinner, is to be a writer. And it is nice to be a writer. "And what does *he* do?" "Why, he writes." It is impossible to say it without shading the voice with awe. There is an air to it, a distinction. The literary Rotarians have helped us and themselves along to the stage where it doesn't matter a damn what you write; where all writers are equal. They can put precisely the same amount of high and sincere excitement into the sentences "Ernest Hemingway has completed another novel" and "Anne Parrish confesses she is having so much fun finishing her new book that she almost cries when she has to leave her desk at bedtime." Perfectly level, always, is the business basis.

There are other ways than luncheons, teas, and banquets for the members of the brotherhood to get their fun, as well as their coffee and cakes. They can organize and run Book Weeks, at popular department stores (to some ways of thinking, if this world were anything near what it should be there would be no more need of a Book Week than there would be of a Society for the Prevention of Cruelty to Children); they can appear in bookshops, to shake hands with the public, or any portion of it; and they can tour the country, to talk to the ladies upon what Ford Madox Ford said about American oysters, and how Fannie Hurst wears her hair. In our smaller towns, the literary lecturer has practically replaced the seamstress-in-by-the-day.

An enviable company, these joiners-up, with good cheer and appreciation for their daily portion. And about them always, like the scent of new violets, is the sweet and reassuring sense of superiority. For, being literary folk, they are licensed to be most awfully snooty about the Babbitts.

February 11, 1928

¶ ANNE PARRISH (1888–1957) had a minor reputation as a novelist; her *All Kneeling* was a favorite of Alexander Woollcott.

Excuse It, Please

When you have to apologize it is well, I suppose, to get the thing over quickly, and then go quietly along about your parlor games. So this week's piece of living literature must start off with the gifted author, thumb in mouth and head hanging like an old catalpa pod, publicly suing for pardon. It is not a comfortable thing to do. We are a proud lot, we mad Varicks.

When Ernest Hemingway's *Men Without Women* was published, I went promptly, sincerely, and, I do think, pardonably wild. That would have been all very sweet and pretty if I had kept it in the sanctity of my hotel room, but no; never the half-measure girl, I had to go leaping into print with my excitement. For Mr. Hemingway, I selected these words: "He is, to me, the greatest living writer of short stories." For his book, I worked up this combination: "I do not know where you can find a finer collection of stories." That's what I said. Loud and clear and cocky, I said it.

Lately I have had a letter (I can feel again my surprise and delight at receiving it, for it is ever like a day in the country to me to find in my mail a plain white envelope, without the name of a collection agency printed in the upper left-hand corner), a patient and courteous letter from a gentleman who quoted my words about *Men Without Women,* and suggested for my attention a book of short stories called *Seven Men*—in especial, he said, the tale "A. V. Laider" contained therein. I read the note with a sickening sensation that threatened to become definite action. "Oh, my God," I said—I was brought up in a mining town, and the old phrases come back in moments of emotion—"I forgot about *Seven Men!*"

That was all I had done. I had only forgotten about *Seven Men.* In my excitement over Ernest Hemingway, all I did was forget about Max Beerbohm.

I thank my correspondent, damn him, for reminding me. Even, in my humility, I sit silent while he says that "A. V. Laider" is the best story in Beerbohm's book, although I am an old "Enoch Soames" girl myself. This is me apologizing. I am a fool, a bird-brain, a liar and a horse-thief. I promise to try to be better; never again will I mess about with such phrases as "greatest living writer" and "do not know where you can find a finer collection." (While I am crawling this far, I had better keep right along and say that another little lapse of memory was my overlooking the fact that Mr. Rudyard Kipling, not only alive but feeling fine, has been no slouch at short-story writing.) I am done. I wouldn't touch a superlative again with an umbrella.

But it would be all right, wouldn't it, if I amended my remarks to read: "Ernest Hemingway is, to me, the greatest living American writer of short stories"? Or maybe this would do better: "Ernest Hemingway is, to me, the greatest living American short-story writer who lives in Paris most of the time but goes to Switzerland to ski, served with the Italian Army during the World War, has been a prize-fighter and has fought bulls, is coming to New York in the spring, is in his early thirties, has a black moustache, and is still waiting for that two hundred francs I lost to him at bridge." Or maybe, after all, the only thing to do is to play safe and whisper: "Ernest Hemingway is, to me, a good writer."

And now that that is done, I'll be getting up off my hands and knees, and doing the week's wash.

February 18, 1928

Our Lady
of the Loudspeaker

It was to be expected, I suppose, that Aimee
Semple McPherson, that Somewhat Different Entertainer, would write a book. Anybody might
have foreseen that that would be. Anybody, that
is, except me. I am the one who believes, when
things are calm and peaceful, that there is a
chance of their staying so. That is the way I have
gone about all my life. I really must make a note
on my desk calendar to have my head examined
one day next week. I am beginning to have more
and more piercing doubts that my fontanel ever
closed up properly.

Well, Aimee Semple McPherson has written a
book, and were you to call it a little peach, you
would not be so much as scratching its surface.
It is the story of her life, and it is called *In the
Service of the King*, which title is perhaps a bit
dangerously suggestive of a romantic novel. It
may be that this autobiography is set down in
sincerity, frankness, and simple effort. It may be,
too, that the Statue of Liberty is situated in Lake
Ontario.

I have never heard Mrs. McPherson preach—
a record which, Heaven helping me, I purpose
keeping untarnished—but from her literary style,

I get the idea. I give you, for your birthday, a typical bit from her opus:

"Quicksand!

"Pernicious quicksand!

"Cloying, treacherous, relentless quicksand!

"The soul-destroying quicksand"—no, no; not "that hung in the well." "The soul-destroying quicksand of unbelief!"

You see? And she can go on like that for hours. Can, hell—does.

On the occasions that she drifts into longer and broader sentences, she writes as many other three-named authoresses have written before. Her manner takes on the thick bloom of rich red plush. The sun becomes "that round orb of day" (as opposed, I expect, to those square orbs you see about so much lately); maple syrup is "Springtide's liquid love gift from the heart of the maple wood"; the forest, by a stroke of inspiration, turns out to be "a cathedral of stately grandeur and never ceasing wonder and awe" (argue, if you will, for "cloying quicksand" as the phrase superb, but me, I'll hold out for "stately grandeur"); the ocean—you'll never guess—is "a broad expanse of sparkling silver"; icy panes are portrayed by the delicate whimsy "Jack Frost had completely painted the windows with his magic brush"; and the gifted author is frequently asking you to "But Hold!" It is difficult to say whether Mrs. McPherson is happier in her crackling exclamations or in her bead-curtain-and-chenille-fringe style. Presumably the lady is happy in both manners. That would make her two up on me.

As for the plot of the work—oh, do sit down; I've got so much to tell you. She starts off with a bang in a chapter called "The Escape." It tells about her return over the desert from that mysterious hut where those two mean men and that big, strong woman had held her for ransom—you remember about that. Lost at night in trackless sand and rustling undergrowth, she prays to be brought to safety. It is here, in her first quoted prayer, that you glimpse Mrs. McPherson's relations with her Maker. She is patient, always, with the Almighty, and explicit, and she is a firm believer in jogging His memory. Thus the prayer of forensic desperation that bubbles from her heart:

"O God, Thou who didst lead the Children of Israel across the wilderness and guide them in all their journeys—Thou who didst provide for them insomuch that they were fed from the skies and watered from the rock, and didst even keep their shoes from wearing out—Thou who didst care for the three Hebrew children, and kept them safe, though cast into the fiery furnace, so that not a hair of their head was singed, nor was the smell of burning upon their garments—Thou who hast ever looked down in pity upon Thy children in their trials—heard and answered their prayers—Thou hast never failed me before and Thou wilt not fail me now—hear my prayer and guide my weary footsteps to safety, for I am lost and sore distressed."

And so she got back to Los Angeles, and—as was later developed at the trial—her shoes were not only kept from wearing out, but were not even scuffed.

But there was trouble awaiting her. Dose ole debbil unbelievers greeted her account of her kidnaping and escape with roars of gay laughter. Reporters and photographers—Mrs. McPherson's bêtes noires—descended upon her and tore her privacy from her; and you know what her privacy means to our little lady. True, the members of her congregation made whoopee in the streets, practically smothered her with roses, and carried her about in a flower-decked chair to celebrate her restoration to them. But it was not enough. "I turned," she says, "toward the window of memory and looked back for respite to the peaceful green meadows of childhood.

"I can see it all now—"

All right, Eddie. Black-out, and into the story of the early life.

She was born in Canada, lived peacefully, went through a couple of pages of doubt, and then decided to go in for saving souls. She married an evangelist named Robert Semple, and went with him to China to convert the natives, a strange, yellow people who put food on the graves of their dead and speak an outlandish language. There Mr. Semple died, and, after her little daughter was born, she returned to the United States, to do mission work. But loneliness took her, and she made a second marriage, to which she devotes one grudging paragraph. "I took up my household duties," she says, "with the understanding that I should go back to the Lord's work if ever the call came." Well, the call came, sharp and clear as if from the whistle of some celestial doorman, and back she went. "My husband," she says, "recognizing the call, went with me and helped me for a time, but decided to go back to his world of business."

And that is the only peep we get at Mr. Mc-
Pherson. I wish that one day he would write the
story of his life; there is a book I should love to
read. Meanwhile, I can only hope that he has
enjoyed a fraction of the success in "his world
of business" that his wife has in hers.

There were years, then, of touring the country
holding revival meetings. Early in her career,
Mrs. McPherson proved herself adept at advertising. In one small town was a poor, drunken
half-wit, the butt of the local jokesters, who
earned a tiny living as town crier. Mrs. McPherson conceived the charming idea of sending him
through the streets, ringing his bell and crying,
"Hear ye! Hear ye! I have given my heart to
Christ. Come down to the revival tonight and hear
Sister McPherson preach about the Christ who
saved even me!"

On another occasion, she arrived in St. Peters-
burg at carnival time, when the streets were
thronged with floats. It looked as if business were
going thus to be taken away from her, but she
thought up a dear little scheme to call herself
to the attention of the romping public. She dressed
up her flivver in leaves and boughs, and erected
upon it an evangelist's tent of sheets, on which
was painted: "Jesus Saves! Repent and be Con-
verted! I'm on the way to the Tent Revival.
R. U.?"

The car was entered in the parade of floats,
and, Mrs. McPherson blushingly admits, was the
wow of the entertainment.

Thus she progressed triumphantly along the
bright way that led to the mighty temple in Los
Angeles. Hers is a story of virtue victorious. Oc-

G   73

casionally she was mildly in need, but never for long; for Heaven—which seems, from Mrs. Mc-Pherson's personal testimony, to be a sort of gold-paved mail-order house—promptly shipped her food, clothing, money, houses, and even canary birds, as she required them. But never did she endure the little daily heartaches, the quarrels and partings and ugliness that are the lot of the rest of us. She dwelt ever in the blissful amity that is the due of the virtuous. (Not even does she dignify by mention that pretty little jam she got into with her mother, at the time of the kidnaping episode.) Never, indeed, have I known an auto-biographer so lavishly to award herself all the breaks.

In the Service of the King has caused an upset in my long-established valuations. With the publication of this, her book, Aimee Semple McPherson has replaced Elsie Dinsmore as my favorite character in fiction.

¶

February 25, 1928

¶ AIMEE SEMPLE MCPHERSON'S story is told in this review, but present-day readers might not know of the newspaper sensation caused by the famous lady evangelist's reported abduction and escape in 1927. . . . The name of ELSIE DINSMORE, the virtuous and put-upon heroine of a series of twenty-six books for girls by Martha Finley (1828–1909), was a byword for all who began to read in the late nineteenth century, and for a generation into this one.

The Compleat Bungler

His publishers say of Mr. George Reith, the author of *The Art of Successful Bidding*, that he, "by virtue of his new position as Chairman of the Card Committee of the Knickerbocker Whist Club, is now the highest authority in the auction bridge world." So you see there is something wrong. Obviously the publishers have never met a certain gentleman who shall be nameless—being already possessed of all the other characteristics of one born out of wedlock—who was my bridge partner last Saturday night. Had they listened to him, they could never have rated Mr. Reith as anything more than second highest authority.

I do not know if my quondam partner was ever chairman of any card committee, and I doubt if he is so much as up for the Knickerbocker Whist Club. There is even some room for argument as to whether or not he was the boy that wrote the game. But it was he who was elected, by an overwhelming vote of one, to expound its principles to all those in darkness. He was Elwell's representative on earth. I would draw him for a partner; one hundred and ten million people in the country, and I would draw him.

My own bridge is of the experimentalist school;

it has been suggested, indeed, that what it really needs are backing from Otto Kahn and stage-settings by John Dos Passos. There is youth to my game, youth and hope and fearlessness and a wild, hungry seeking. People have been known to gather from blocks around, to stand back of my chair and puzzle out just what it all meant. High have run the bets as to precisely what I was playing, with the speculations ranging all the way from Authors to Prisoners' Base. You can see that mine is no ordinary, patterned, box-office bridge. It is more a symbol of life, really, than a game of cards. Why, I have ever asked, be a slave to form? Look at Cézanne. Is he a slave? Is he shackled to conventions? Is he afraid of the laughter of the herd? Is he untrue to his gift? Is he mineral? Is he in this room?

Emotionally, I am a bridge-player of the manic-depressive type. If I can get all the way through a rubber without once mistaking a spade for a club, I want to go right up and slap Milton Work on the back. If, on the other hand, my partner gives me a dirty, even a slightly soiled, look, I am broken for the evening, and all my thoughts are of the emptiness of life and the sweet solace of the grave. And my partner at last Saturday night's lynching-bee began bestowing positively insanitary looks upon me, even before I had finished my first deal. (All right, suppose I did spill seven or eight cards on the floor. That doesn't make me any less a fellow creature, with blood and bones and an immortal soul and decent, human feelings, does it?)

He turned out to be one of those icily patient boys; he did a good deal of deep sighing, and of asking me, in an heroically mild voice, such questions as "Would you mind telling me what was your idea in leading me a diamond? Or is it a secret?" I kept back the tears, however, like a little soldier, until that moment in our last rubber—our last rubber on earth, undoubtedly—when he suggested that he and the others stop playing and just sit back and watch me do my card tricks.

It was those words that led me to take steps about leashing my bridge game to the standards of the mob. I was advised to study Mr. Reith's *The Art of Successful Bidding*. They told me that it was sane, simple, instructive, and authoritative. I do not question that it is all those things; it is, I have no moment's doubt, a fine textbook. But it is well over my head. I can't even jump for it. There is no use in my poring over advanced stuff, when what I am seeking is some simple, kindly, one-syllabled formula for the way to remember What's Out.

However, the book has done one great thing to salve my ego. In the blurb on its dust-cover, it is stated: "His book is entirely unusual. Any ordinary bridge-player will find he can study it without a deck of cards and he will improve his game." So now I have found out what I am. I am no ordinary bridge-player—can Whitehead say more? It is comforting, it is heartening to know, on the highest authority, a thing like that about oneself. I am no ordinary bridge-player. Say I'm weary, say I'm sad, say that health and wealth have missed me, say I'm growing old, but add I'm no ordinary bridge-player. And if I ever see that Saturday-night boy again, God forbid, I'll take no more cracks about card tricks out of him.

Well, now that that is settled for all time, there
are better things to be done. There is a good
book out. It is *Home to Harlem*, the first novel
by Claude McKay, who has written no prose, to
my knowledge, before this. It is a rough book; a
bitter, blunt, cruel, bashing novel. I cannot quite
pull myself to the point of agreeing with those
who hail it as a wholly fine work. It seems to me
that there are parts of it that do not come off;
I feel, a little uncomfortably, that Mr. McKay
has not yet found himself as a novelist. ("Do not
come off" and "found himself," both in one sentence! Tie that for coining phrases, if you can.)
There are times when his style is regrettably close
to that of Miss Fannie Hurst, and there is, of
course, his debt—part of what is rapidly assuming
the proportions of a National Debt—to the manner of Ernest Hemingway. But it is a good book,
and I have yet to see the reader who can put it
down once he has opened it.

We needed, and we needed badly, a book about
Harlem Negroes by a Negro. White men can
write, and have written, Heaven knows, such tales,
but one never loses consciousness, while reading
them, of the pallor of the authors' skins. Mr. Mc-
Kay's novel seems to me a vitally important addition to American letters. And for his easily
achieved feat of putting even further into their
place the writings of Mr. Carl Van Vechten, I
shall be grateful to him from now on.

March 17, 1928

¶ Joseph Elwell, a leading authority on bridge, was
found murdered in 1920—a crime still unsolved.

Ethereal Mildness

Oh, I feel terrible. Rotten, I feel. I've got Spring Misery. I've got a mean attack of Crocus Urge. I bet you I'm running a temperature right at this moment; running it ragged. I ought to be in bed, that's where I ought to be. Not that it would do any good if I were. I can't sleep. I can't sleep for a damn. I can't sleep for sour apples. I can't sleep for you and who else.

I'm always this way in the Spring. Sunk in Springtime: or Take Away Those Violets. I hate the filthy season. Summer makes me drowsy, Autumn makes me sing, Winter's pretty lousy, but I hate Spring. They know how I feel. They know what Spring makes out of me. Just a Thing That Was Once a Woman, that's all I am in the Springtime. But do they do anything about it? Oh, no. Not they. Every year, back Spring comes, with the nasty little birds yapping their fool heads off, and the ground all mucked up with arbutus. Year after year after year. And me not able to sleep, on account of misery. All right, Spring. Go ahead and laugh your girlish laughter, you big sap. Funny, isn't it? People with melancholic insomnia are screams, aren't they? You just go on and laugh yourself simple. That's the girl!

It isn't as if I hadn't tried practically every way I ever heard of to induce sleep. I've taken long walks around the room in the midnight silence, and I've thought soothing thoughts, and I've recited long passages of poetry; I have even tried counting Van Dorens. But nothing works, drugs nor anything else. Not poppy nor mandragora. There was a book called *Not Poppy,* and now there's one called *Not Magnolia,* and is it any wonder a person goes crazy? What with Spring and book titles and loss of sleep, acute melancholia is the least I could have. I'm having a bad time. Oh, awful.

There has been but one sweet, misty interlude in my long stretch of white nights. That was the evening I fell into a dead dreamless slumber brought on by the reading of a book called *Appendicitis.* (Well, picture my surprise when this turned out to be a book review, after all! You could have knocked me over with a girder.) *Appendicitis* is the work of Thew Wright, A.B., M.D., F.A.C.S., who has embellished his pages with fascinatingly anatomical illustrations, and has remarked, in his dedication, that he endeavors through this book to bring an understanding of appendicitis to the laity. And it is really terribly hard to keep from remarking, after studying the pictures, "That was no laity; that's my wife." It is hard, but I'll do it if it kills me.

You might, and with good reasons, take for your favorite picture the "Front View of Abdominal Cavity." It is good, I admit; it has nice nuances, there is rhythm to the composition, and clever management is apparent in the shadows.

But my feeling is that it is a bit sentimental, a little pretty-pretty, too obviously done with an eye toward popularity. It may well turn out to be another "Whistler's Mother" or a "Girl With Fan." My own choice is the impression of "Vertical Section of Peritoneum." It has strength, simplicity, delicacy, pity, and irony. Perhaps, I grant you, my judgment is influenced by my sentiment for the subject. For who that has stood, bareheaded, and beheld the Peritoneum by moonlight can gaze unmoved upon its likeness?

The view of the Peritoneum induces waking dreams, but not slumber. For that I had to get into the text of the book. In his preface, Dr. Wright observes that "The chapter on anatomy, while it may appear formidable, will, it is believed, well repay the reader for his effort in reading it." Ever anxious to be well repaid, I turned to the chapter. It did appear formidable; it appeared as formidable as all get-out. And when I saw that it started "Let us divide the abdominal cavity into four parts by means of four imaginary lines," I could only murmur, "Ah, let's don't. Surely we can think up something better to play than that."

From there, I went skipping about through the book, growing ever more blissfully weary. Only once did I sit up sharply, and dash sleep from my lids. That was at the section having to do with the love-life of poisonous bacteria. That, says the author, "is very simple and consists merely of the bacterium dividing into two equal parts." Think of it—no quarrels, no lies, no importunate telegrams, no unanswered letters. Just peace and sunshine and quiet evenings around the lamp. Probably bacteria sleep like logs. Why shouldn't they? What is Spring to them?

And, at the end of twenty-four hours, the happy couple—or the happy halves, if you'd rather—will have 16,772,216 children to comfort them in their old age. Who would not be proud to have 16,772,216 little heads clustered about his knee, who would not be soothed and safe to think of the young people carrying on the business after the old folks have passed on? I wish, I wish I were a poisonous bacterium. Yes, and I know right now where I'd go to bring up my family, too. I've got that all picked out. What a time I'd show *him!*

Barring the passages dealing with the life and times of bacteria, there is nothing in Dr. Wright's work to block repose. It is true that I never did find out whether I really had appendicitis—which is why I ever started the book, anyway—or whether it was just the effects of that new Scotch of mine which, friends tell me, must have been specially made by the Borgias. But *Appendicitis* gave me a few blessed hours of forgetfulness, and for that I am almost cringingly grateful to Thew Wright, A.B., M.D., F.A.C.S., and all-around good fellow.

❡ I didn't have such luck with George Jean Nathan's *Art of the Night.* In fact, it acted upon me like so much black coffee, and this in spite of the fact that any book with "Art" in its title usually renders me unconscious as soon as I've cracked it.

In several reviews of his book that I have seen, his critics have taken Mr. Nathan to task—and taking Mr. Nathan to task ranks as a productive pastime with beating the head against a granite wall—for repeating himself. I cannot see that this is so grave a charge. Mr. Nathan has written many books on the theatre, his convictions are always his convictions, and they are invariably present in his writings. This would not seem to be unintentional, so far as I can fathom. Perhaps he emphasizes the same points that he has long been emphasizing, but he has always something more to say on them, and he always has new points to make.

Art of the Night, it seems to me, is the most valuable of his works on the theatre, as well as the most entertaining. The piece called "Advice to a Young Critic," though it be frequently phrased in flippancy, is deeply sound and thoughtful, and the paper on "Writers of Plays" highly important. Mr. Nathan has his enthusiasms, but they do not attack his control, as do the penchants of many of our other dramatic critics besiege theirs, causing them to produce not so much compilations of critical papers as bundles of fragrant love-letters. George Jean Nathan does his selected subject the courtesy of knowing about it. He writes of it brilliantly, bravely, and authoritatively. He can, in short, write. And so he makes almost all of the other dramatic commentators (I can think, in fact, of but three exceptions, and I'm not sure of two of those) look as if they spelled out their reviews with alphabet blocks.

So I couldn't, you see, find even a wink of sleep in *Art of the Night.* And I couldn't, either, in James Stephens' *Etched in Moonlight,* a collection of his strange, sad, beautiful stories. The slow, relentless agony of the story he names

"Hunger" will, indeed, probably keep me awake from now until Summer comes. It is a superb story; but it was just the thing to undo any pitiful little trifles of good I had picked up for myself, and throw me right back into galloping Spring Misery. Oh, I'm sunk.

Spring. Yeah. Spring.

March 24, 1928

¶ Currently famous, among others, were CARL VAN DOREN, historian and author of *Benjamin Franklin*; MARK VAN DOREN, his brother, the poet; IRITA VAN DOREN (then Carl's wife), editor of the *New York Herald Tribune* "Books." . . . GEORGE JEAN NATHAN (1882–1958), the drama critic, was writing in *The New Yorker* at this time, after having been associated with H. L. Mencken in editing the magazines *Smart Set* and *The American Mercury*.

Mr. Lewis Lays It On with a Trowel

In the combined names of Social Intercourse, Meeting Interesting People, and Getting Out of a Rut, I have taken, in my time, some terrible beatings. I have listened to poets rendering their own odes. I have had the plots of yet unwritten plays given me in tiniest detail, I have assisted in charades, I have been politely mystified by card tricks, I have even been sent out of the room and been forced, on my return, to ask the assembled company such questions as I hoped might reveal to me what Famous Character in Fiction they represented. I have spent entire evenings knee-deep in derry-down-derries, listening to quaint old English ballads done without accompaniment; I have been backed into cold corners by pianos while composers showed me how that thing they wrote three years before Gershwin did "The Man I Love" went; I know a young man who has an inlaid ukelele. You see these gray hairs? Well, making whoopee with the intelligentsia was the way I earned them.

But, strait though my gate has been and charged with punishment my scroll, there is one licking I have yet to take. I have never heard Mr. Sinclair Lewis recite the monologues which make up his new book, *The Man Who Knew Coolidge.* I know that he performs this feat, for Dr. Henry Seidel Canby says so in his review of the book, and Dr. Canby would be the last one to tease a person. But for me, thus far, Mr. Lewis's monologues exist only on the printed page. And that way lies the silver lining. It is no breach of manners to close a book before its end is reached.

I have, at the moment, a friend who is trying to make a lady out of me, and the first step in the uphill climb has been the gaining of my promise to keep from employing certain words. So I can't tell you that I think *The Man Who Knew Coolidge,* whether regarded as an entertainment, a portrait, a contribution to American letters, or as all three, is rotten. I could say that if I could use the word "rotten," but I can't use the word "rotten." The question of honor is involved. I gave my solemn pledge that I wouldn't say "rotten" any more. "Rotten" is not a nice word for a lady to use. It sounds lousy.

But I can say—and, if you don't mind, I will— that I think Mr. Lewis's latest work is as heavy-handed, clumsy, and dishonest a burlesque as it has been my misfortune to see in years. I say it, I admit, waiting for a bolt of lightning to come and flatten me permanently, for it is dangerous business for the likes of me to go about saying harsh things of Sinclair Lewis. Two of our most literary literary critics have already gone wild, in a booksy way, over *The Man Who Knew Coolidge,* and, though I have not yet seen any words of Mr. Mencken's on it, he printed the first piece in the book in his *American Mercury.* I am trembling like a what's-this leaf for my presumption, but I stick to my story.

It seems to me that *The Man Who Knew Coolidge* is Babbitt broadened by a mile, and Babbitt, Lord knows, was never instanced as an exercise in the subtle. Mr. Lewis is no longer the reporter; he has become the parodist. Doubtless it is all very well to sacrifice honesty and accuracy for the sake of comic effect, but when the comic effect doesn't come off, then where are you? Well, of course you are, and a pretty uncomfortable place to be, too.

I have been one who has for years marched under a banner inscribed "Sinclair Lewis for Pope." I think he is of vast importance. To my mind *Main Street* and *Babbitt* are invaluable historical documents. It seems to me that *Arrowsmith* belongs with the few American novels that have real magnificence. And *Elmer Gantry*—well, they say it's great. I never told anybody this in my life before, and please, for Heaven's sake, don't get it around, but I couldn't read *Elmer Gantry*. I simply could not read it. I know that is a shocking confession to make, and I shall undoubtedly fry in hell for my failure, but there you are. Now you know the worst, or maybe it's the second worst, about me.

But I am not a bit ashamed to admit my inability to finish *The Man Who Knew Coolidge*. (All right, lightning; what are you going to do about it? Let's see you knock this typewriter out from under me, if you think you're so good.) It is to me, because of its deliberate untruth, an outrageously irritating book. It is not caricature; it is absolute misrepresentation. I hold not even the briefest brief for the Babbittry, but there was never any one as bad as Mr. Lewis's hundred-percent American, Lowell Schmaltz. The more I think of it, the madder I get. I am in a fair way towards getting on into what is locally known as "one of those spells of hers."

I wish I could say "rotten." You don't know how much I need to say it.

April 7, 1928

These Much Too Charming People

And so the butterfly days are over. For me, there shall be no more lolling in the sweet, pale sunshine, no more laughing and singing and using words in sentences through the dear and fragrant little hours of the night, no more getting up in the steely noons with a hangover that ought to be in the Smithsonian Institution, under glass. I have flung the last of my roses, roses, riotously before the throng. I have gone earnest. I have a purpose. I have a Cause. My white plume, please, Meadows, and tell them to have my favorite charger at the door in ten minutes.

My life and my arms are now and hereafter consecrated to the services of the Society for the Abolition of Charm. It would be advisable, perhaps, for the Society to make a drive for new members; for, thus far, I am the president, vice-president, secretary, board of directors, list of members, and greens committee, and there is such a thing as keeping an organization too exclusive. Yet there is little reason to fear that the Society will pine and die for want of new blood, for surely there must be countless numbers of strong and restless souls who are so good and sick of con-

scious charm that they would willingly drop
everything and join in the movement for its stamp-
ing-out. There is entirely too much charm around,
and something must be done to stop it.

For a time, I was passive about the thing. I
came up against all the better-known varieties of
charm in succession—the wistful, the hearty, the
puckish, the sparkling, the shy, the naïve (that's
the kind I should like to get after first, if it's all
right with you), the mysterious, the dry, the
sporadic, the quaint, and the Purely Physical—
and took them meekly as part of the fardels to
which we all are heir.

But then it began to get a little thick and sticky.
Everywhere I looked, I saw people going charming. Charm flowed like water, and appeared to be
turned on and off in the manner of the same
necessary liquid. I couldn't get away from it; the
only place I was safe from charm was in my own
bed, and you know yourself you do have to get
out of bed once in a while, if only to see what
the headlines say. My first idea was to flee the
whole works, and escape to some mountain fast-
ness, some wild and thunderous pass—I was holding out, I recall, for a spot called Rising Gorge as
appropriate to my condition—where These Over-
Charming People would never penetrate. But that
would have been the deed of a coward, and though
we may ride hard, we mad Marches, and lie and
swear and raise cheques, there are two things we
cannot do: we never resist an officer (or a private)
and we never turn yellow.

The thing to do was to face the evil, and strive
to wipe it out. That was how I got into my Cause.

Then and there was born the Society for the Abolition of Charm. It has not yet been definitely decided how the Society is to go about its work of banishing charm from the face of the earth, but as soon as there are some more members we might meet out in back of the barn and see what can be done.

An event that speeded up the founding of the Society was the publication of Miss G. B. Stern's ¶ novel, *Debonair*. The book takes its faintly revolting title from its hero's conception of its heroine. Thus does he think of her, and thus, I regret to say, does he address her. So, in like manner, did I ever have a beau he might ponder on me and apostrophize me as "Shiftless." ·

I yield to nobody that I can think of in my admiration for Miss Stern. She is, I think, a fine and sharp and skillful writer. It has been ever a source of sad amazement to me that there was not international screaming over her *The Dark Gentleman,* which is as delicate and shrewd a satire as I know, and the best dog story I have ever read. (I wish that the last bit of that sentence were higher praise, for, though I am one who turns practically faint with love at the sight of a dog a block away, the usual uplifting tale of the noble beast who gives his life for his master, his master's girl-friend, or his master's enemy, according to the powers of the author, is a thing that I am utterly unable to spell out.) Miss Stern wrote of her dogs without coquetry, sentimentality, or brutality, thus establishing a record. Her dogs were none of your cold, pure, brave, noble beasts, and so their doings were absorbing reading; well, you know—it's the same way with books about people who are not all cold, pure, brave, and noble. It is a thorn to me that nothing much is done about *The Dark Gentleman.* I knew of few who had heard of it; and I know of none to whom I have suggested it who ever wants to read much of anything else.

Oh, I beg your pardon. I was supposed to be talking about *Debonair,* wasn't I? Well, it seems to me that in this latest book of hers, Miss Stern has had that thing happen to her which befalls most fine satirists. By the nature of her gift, she writes superbly of the people she hates; but when she tries to do a character whom she likes and wishes her readers to like, the result is appalling.

The heroine of *Debonair*—her name is Loveday, which, looked at from any angle, is pretty hard to do with—is one of those charming girls. Indeed, she is so full of charm that she is practically panting with it. Now charm is bad enough to meet with in daily life as we were saying not five minutes ago, but God deliver you and me from charm on paper. I have yet to have an author inform me that a character is charming, and then, by that character's deeds and conversation, convince me of the fact.

Loveday—would you mind if I referred to her simply as "L."? I have my health to think of—is one of those cute, cute, cute, reckless, scatter-brained, daring, but golden-hearted young women that always make me want to get out the trusty old gun that Grandpa carried all through the Civil War without firing a shot. Oh, how gaily and irresponsibly she does rattle on, all during the book! "Happy me!" she calls herself, and she addresses her mother as "Lamb-bird." Then she has a little way of saying "quee" instead of "queer," and there is one occasion when she employs "pew" rather than use the less whimsical "pure." In short, I cannot tell you how not hungry it makes me to follow her conversation. "Debonair" may be her lover's word for her, but "God-awful" will ever be her nickname with me.

There is unfortunately so very much of L. in the book—and it's quee how little of that pew young thing is enough to last you a lifetime—that you close it with her alone in your mind. And that is too bad, for in *Debonair* Miss Stern has done, out of her bright and exquisite bitterness, two fine portraits—those of L.'s mother, and of the mother of the hero. L.'s mother seems to me a little less successful than the other; she is the silver cord lady, portrayed unerringly at first, but, as the book progresses, gone over into exaggeration. But the hero's mother, Petal—"Petal-to-my-Friends"; "Petal—it suits her"—that sweet, fragile, beloved, gentle devil of a woman, is, I think, as true and sure and skilled a portrayal as I have seen in twenty years of hard reading.

I wish, so that a fine novel need not have been betrayed, that *Debonair* could have been done without its title role. But there is a little comfort to be had from the quee young lady. Read about her, and you will immediately send in your application for membership in the Society for the Abolition of Charm. That girl will do much to put the Society on its feet.

Put the white plume back in the cupboard,

Meadows, if you please. Miss Stern's Loveday is taking over my work for the Cause.

April 21, 1928

¶ G. B. STERN (1890–), the British novelist, was already held in high regard for her *Matriarch* series of novels of a Jewish family.

Duces Wild

Signor Benito Mussolini, back in the days when he was wearing white shirts, if any, wrote a book. It has lately been translated into English and stacked high on the local book-counters. It is called *The Cardinal's Mistress*. Just when you think that things are beginning to break a little better, it turns out that Mussolini has been writing books about prelates' girl-friends. That's the way life is. That's how things are managed in this world of yours. Sometimes I think I'll give up trying, and just go completely Russian and sit on a stove and moan all day.

It is rumored that Il Duce is having one of those old-fashioned Latin tantrums over the translation and publication of his literary gem. That would be, for me, the one bit of cheer in the whole performance. Anything that makes Mussolini sore is velvet so far as I am concerned. If only I had a private income, I would drop everything right now, and devote the scant remainder of my days to teasing the Dictator of All Italy. If anybody comes up to you on the street and tells you that he is my favorite character in history, would you mind saying it's all a black lie? I want to scotch any rumor that I am what Mr. Walter Winchell would call "that way" about him. Indeed, my dream-life is largely made up of scenes in which I say to him, "Oh, Il Duce, yourself, you big stiff," and thus leave him crushed to a pulp.

The Cardinal's Mistress was written when Mussolini was a cunning little shaver of twenty-six, at which time he was secretary to the Socialist Chamber of Labor. His salary was twenty-four dollars a month and the use of the parlor, and he eked it out—he has never been a heavy eker—by giving French lessons and pursuing literature. For this book, first published serially, he thought up the title, *Claudia Particella, l'Amante del Cardinale: Grande Romanzo dei Tempi del Cardinale Emanuel Madruzzo*. Well do I know, from reading the newspapers, that those who attempt disagreement with the Dictator trifle with their health; so I shall but remark, in a quiet way, that if *The Cardinal's Mistress* is a *grande romanzo*, I am Alexandre Dumas, *père et fils*.

On the memorable day that *The Cardinal's Mistress* arrived in the office of this lucky magazine, I was the girl who pled, "Please teacher, may I have it to take home with me? Honest, I don't want a cent of money for reviewing it. I'll do it free of charge; I'll even pay handsomely for the privilege." Well, of course, they wouldn't hear a word of that—or at least I hope to heaven they didn't—but I got the book. I had all sorts of happy plans about it. I was going to have a lot of fun. I was going to kid what you Americans call the tripe (*les tripes*) out of it. At last, I thought, had come my big chance to show up this guy Mussolini. A regular Roman holiday, that's what it was going to be.

Well, the joke was on me. There will be little kidding out of me on the subject of the Mussolini masterpiece, for I am absolutely unable to read my way through it. I tried—the Lord knows I tried. I worked, to employ the most inept simile in the language, like a dog. I put on my oldest clothes (first carefully hanging my second oldest in the cupboard), denied myself to my bill-collectors, backed the bureau against the door, and set myself to my task. And I got just exactly nowhere with that book. From the time I cracked its covers to that whirling moment, much later, when I threw myself exhausted on my bed, it had me licked. I couldn't make head, tail, nor good red herring of the business.

In fairness to the author—and I would strip a gear any time in an effort to be square toward that boy—it is in my line of duty to admit that with any book on the general lines of *The Cardinal's Mistress,* I start 'way back of scratch. When I am given a costume romance beginning, "From the tiny churches hidden within the newly budding verdure of the valleys, the evensong of the Ave Maria floated gently forth and died upon the lake," my only wish is that I, too, might float gently forth and die, and I'm not particular whether it's upon the lake or on dry land. I go on to read of a lady whose "half-closed eyes understood the sorcery of poisonous passions," and my one longing is to close those eyes all the way for her. And then I get into a mess of characters named the Count di Castelnuovo and Don Benizio and Carl Emanuel Madruzzo, Cardinal and Archbishop of Trent and secular prince of the Trentino, and Filiberta, and Madonna Claudia—and everything goes black before my eyes. I know that I am never going to understand who is who and what side they are on, and I might just as well give up the unequal struggle.

There seems to be a lot of things going on in *The Cardinal's Mistress*. There are political intrigues, and subtle poisons, and broken-hearted novices dying in convents, and mysterious horsemen dashing away in clouds of dust, and appropriate characters in history, and all the rest of that stock company. But such things are not for me. Even when they are fairly good, the Sandman has me, before I have so much as reached the middle of them.

For me, the one good bit of the book is its preface by Hiram Motherwell (he also translated the novel). Mr. Motherwell writes his introduction with an irreproachable seriousness, almost a solemnity, in his bearing toward Il Duce as a literary figure; and yet there is that something about it which makes the thoughtful reader feel that the translator would be just as well off if he kept out of the uncertain Italian climate for a time. It is to be hoped that he decides on some nice, faraway place—such as New York City, say—as the ideal winter resort.

Weak though the ordeal has left me, I shall never be the one to grudge the time and effort I put into my attempts at reading *The Cardinal's Mistress*. The book has considerably enlarged that dream-life I was telling you about a few minutes ago. It has broadened now to admit that scene in which I tell Mussolini, "And what's more, you can't even write a book that anyone could read.

You old Duce, you." You can see for yourself how flat that would leave him.

There are, as you are not the only one who has been thinking, better things to talk about than the literary output of Benito ("Little Bennie") Mussolini, the Nathalia Crane of Italy. One of the very much better things is *All Kneeling*, Miss Anne Parrish's new novel. It is a quick and deft and constantly amusing satire, the portrait of a lady who so sharply suggests almost all other ladies that you get a little bit frightened. Some years ago, Miss Parrish wrote a book called *A Pocketful of Poses*, which was a promise of what she would some day do in the way of a shrewd and merciless exposal of a pretentious, terrible, and victorious woman. *All Kneeling* is the performance. It is true that the book is occasionally over-written, that certain points are hammered rather too heavily. But, as I was saying to the landlord only this morning, you can't have everything.

September 15, 1928

¶ NATHALIA CRANE (1913–) had a meteoric reputation as a prodigy when her poems, written before the age of eleven, were published in 1924.

Far from Well

The more it
SNOWS-tiddely-pom,
The more it
GOES-tiddely-pom
The more it
GOES-tiddely-pom
On
Snowing.

And nobody
KNOWS-tiddely-pom,
How cold my
TOES-tiddely-pom
How cold my
TOES-tiddely-pom
Are
Growing.

The above lyric is culled from the fifth page of
Mr. A. A. Milne's new book, *The House at Pooh
Corner*, for, although the work is in prose,
there are frequent droppings into more cadenced
whimsy. This one is designated as a "Hum," that
pops into the head of Winnie-the-Pooh as he is
standing outside Piglet's house in the snow, jump-

ing up and down to keep warm. It "seemed to him a Good Hum, such as is Hummed Hopefully to Others." In fact, so Good a Hum did it seem that he and Piglet started right out through the snow to Hum It Hopefully to Eeyore. Oh, darn—there I've gone and given away the plot. Oh, I could bite my tongue out.

As they are trotting along against the flakes, Piglet begins to weaken a bit.

" 'Pooh,' he said at last and a little timidly, because he didn't want Pooh to think he was Giving In, 'I was just wondering. How would it be if we went home now and *practised* your song, and then sang it to Eeyore tomorrow—or—or the next day, when we happen to see him.'

" 'That's a very good idea, Piglet,' said Pooh. 'We'll practise it now as we go along. But it's no good going home to practise it, because it's a special Outdoor Song which Has To Be Sung In The Snow.'

" 'Are you sure?' asked Piglet anxiously.

" 'Well, you'll see, Piglet, when you listen. Because this is how it begins. *The more it snows, tiddely-pom—*'

" 'Tiddely what?' said Piglet." (He took, as you might say, the very words out of your correspondent's mouth.)

" 'Pom,' said Pooh. 'I put that in to make it more hummy.' "

And it is that word "hummy," my darlings, that marks the first place in *The House at Pooh Corner* at which Tonstant Weader Fwowed up.

October 20, 1928

Wallflower's Lament

It has lately been drawn to your correspondent's attention that, at social gatherings, she is not the human magnet she would be. Indeed, it turns out that as a source of entertainment, conviviality, and good fun, she ranks somewhere between a sprig of parsley and a single ice-skate. It would appear, from the actions of the assembled guests, that she is about as hot company as a night nurse.

I don't mean that these facts have been pointed out to her in so many words. Not as yet; although there is a fair chance that a certain young gentleman of her acquaintance, who gets the frankies after the fourth *anis de loso* and goes around telling people what makes them so terrible, will shortly be sitting by her side and beginning, "Look, you know what's the matter with you?" Thus far, she has drawn her deductions from the fact that the invitations have been dying off like flies; so that most of her evenings are given to powdering her friends' backs or straightening their ties, as the case may be, saying, "Now have a good time and be sure to tell me who was there," waving by-by smilingly, and then settling down for a hearty attack of the left-all-alone-again yips. On such occasions as she does make those parties where the hosts apparently assemble the list of guests by drawing names out of a hat, she sits in a corner with her thoughts, smiling brightly the while in order to indicate a pathetic willingness to play; or else she listens to something that used to be in the S.O.S. explain, with the aid of paper and a gold pencil, the course of the war from April 7, 1917, until the late afternoon of Armistice Day. So, being one who can take a hint after the first thirty repetitions, she is now conceding her flop, and retiring constructively from society. Do you know anyone who would want a comparatively young woman—young as compared with the Grand Canyon, for instance—fairly free, and looks white under electric light, to sit up with the children evenings, and let the nurse go out?

It is not that she has not tried to improve her condition before acknowledging its hopelessness. (Oh, come on, let's get the hell out of this, and get into the first person.) I have sought, by study, to better my form and make myself Society's Darling. You see, I had been fed, in my youth, a lot of old wives' tales about the way men would instantly forsake a beautiful woman to flock about a brilliant one. It is but fair to say that, after getting out in the world, I had never seen this happen, but I thought that maybe I might be the girl to start the vogue. I would become brilliant. I would sparkle. I would hold whole dinner tables spellbound. I would have throngs fighting to come within hearing distance of me while the weakest, elbowed mercilessly to the outskirts, would cry, "What did she say?" or "Oh, please ask her to tell it again." That's what I would do. Oh, I could just hear myself.

So I got a book called *Favorite Jokes of Famous People* and settled down to read it, memorize its gems, and repeat them at select gatherings. And from the time of the world's première of my recital until this very living moment, I haven't had an evening off my hands.

It was doubtless ill-advised for me, a very tyro —or, at least, a pretty tyro—as a raconteuse to start off with the selection given in the book as the favorite of Mr. Bruce Barton, a selection which, by the way, could scarcely be classified as "The Joke Nobody Knows." Thus does Mr. Barton begin his chosen story:

"In the pre-prohibition days two young men set forth one evening from Detroit in an automobile. Awakening the next morning, after a somewhat tempestuous night, they found themselves parked in front of a large building which they assumed to be a hotel but was in fact a sanitarium. The proprietor of the institution was not only a vegetarian, but a zealous member of a religious order."

That, you will admit, is a rough start for the amateur story-teller. You have to remember practically everything except your stance. Pre-prohibition, Detroit, two young men, automobile, next morning, hotel which wasn't a hotel, proprietor who was not only a vegetarian but a member of a religious order—that's advanced stuff. It is perhaps sufficient to say that I made a fool of the anecdote. I represented the two young men as coming from Fort Wayne.

Since then, I have had no heart for *Favorite Jokes of Famous People*. I can't even do much about reading it in moments of leisure. The book has been compiled by Frank Nicholson, who dedicates it to "A famous man whose favorite joke is not included in this collection . . . he did not choose to pun," so you can see that he is just the boy who was cut out to collect the best in humor. Mr. Nicholson adds his own touches in giving brief biographies of each celebrity who is represented—one recalls perhaps most sharply his dainty line in his Gene Tunney piece: "Gene says if he gets married he'll quit fighting. What an optimist that guy is!"—which is my entrant for the 1928 Pulitzer prize for the *mot* doing most to advance American manners and standards of culture. It is to be guessed, too, that Mr. Nicholson does not confine his authoring to the biographies; here and there it seems as if he must have crashed into the jokes themselves. For example, in Donald Ogden Stewart's favorite story, the magnificent epic of the horse that sat on eggs, Mr. Nicholson has Mr. Stewart referring to "that blankety blank horse." It has been my privilege to have known Mr. Stewart since he wore sailorsuits—he was in the navy during the war—and never yet have I heard him use any such expression as "blankety blank." Or, at least, certainly not in the presence of any woman.

Out of *Favorite Jokes of Famous People* comes one ray of light, one breath of strange, new fragrance, one cool and silver star. That is the selection given by Mr. Ring Lardner. It is too frail, too exquisite to reproduce here, though I can scarcely tear myself away from quoting it. And it is a source of perpetual amazement that Mr. Frank Ernest Nicholson, author of "What an optimist that guy is!," could have admitted this white violet to his collection. Probably he figured out some meaning to the masterpiece, and will never, never realize that it was Mr. Lardner at his sublime best, in the act of kidding the living tripe out of all such collections of famous things of famous whose-thises.

Well—to get back to me as quickly as possible— when Our Heroine found that she was the bust of the season as a wit and an elocutionist, she decided to turn to that good old stand-by, sex. "Let others raconteur if they will," I said, "but gangway while I go Garbo!" To that end, I acquired a book called *The Technique of the Love Affair,* by one who signs herself "A Gentlewoman," and set out to learn how to loop the Usual Dancing Men.

I have thought, in times past, that I had been depressed. I have regarded myself as one who had walked hand-in-hand with sadness. But until I read that book, depression, as I knew it, was still in its infancy. I have found out, from its pages, that never once have I been right. Never once. Not even one little time.

You know how you ought to be with men? You should always be aloof, you should never let them know you like them, you must on no account let them feel that they are of any importance to you, you must be wrapped up in your own concerns, you may never let them lose sight of the fact that you are superior, you must be, in short, a regular stuffed chemise. And if you could see what I've been doing!

Despite its abominable style and its frequent sandy stretches, *The Technique of the Love Affair* makes, I am bitterly afraid, considerable sense. If only it had been written and placed in my hands years ago, maybe I could have been successful, instead of just successive.

November 17, 1928

¶ BRUCE BARTON: see note for page 17. . . . GENE TUNNEY, who won the World Heavyweight Boxing Championship from Jack Dempsey in 1926, was also known for his literary interests as a student and disciple of William Lyon Phelps. . . . DONALD OGDEN STEWART (1894–), man-about-town, author of humorous books and plays and later of movie scripts, was a member with Dorothy Parker of the Algonquin Round Table group.

And Again,
Mr. Sinclair Lewis

The industry of Mr. Sinclair Lewis is a thing to marvel at, to ponder of a white night, and, if such is your way, to hoist high as an example. To my own admittedly slanted vision, industry ranks with such sour and spinster virtues as thrift, punctuality, level-headedness, and caution. I think that Aldous Huxley utters the loud truth when he says, in *Point Counter Point,* that industry can never substitute for talent. There exists, especially in the American mind, a sort of proud confusion between the two. A list of our authors who have made themselves most beloved and, therefore, most comfortable financially, shows that it is our national joy to mistake for the first-rate, the fecund rate.

Ah, I thought that that was going to turn out better. Oh, dear . . .

Anyhow, the industry of Mr. Lewis is not short of marvelous. There are times, such as after reading *The Man Who Knew Coolidge* and after accomplishing the long trek through the major part of his latest book, *Dodsworth,* when one feels that it might be set to higher purposes; properly hitched up, say, it might supply heat, light, and power to the whole Middle West. It is an almost terrifying force. Think what the man—the man who had behind him such stupendous feats of labor as *Main Street* and *Arrowsmith* and *Elmer Gantry*—has done in this last year. There was *The Man Who Knew Coolidge,* like it or not, there were countless pieces for the weeklies and for the Sunday magazine sections of the newspapers, there was the aching grind of all that posing for all those rotogravure pictures of the honeymoon trip through rural England in the caravan, and now there is a new novel of three hundred and seventy-seven closely printed pages. Three hundred and seventy-seven pages. And I, after the creative labors involved in composing a telegram to the effect that I won't be able to come to dinner Thursday on account of a severe cold, have to go and lie down for the rest of the day.

It is difficult for me to pass upon *Dodsworth.* I find myself in the unenviable position of the early crocus. As I toss and turn at my typewriter —I shouldn't have drunk that coffee—no reviews of the novel have yet appeared. And how am I to know, until I have read the Book Supplement of the New York Sunday *Times,* whether or not this is a truly important work? I cannot, with the slightest sureness, tell you if it will sweep the country, like *Main Street,* or bring forth yards of printed praise, as did *Elmer Gantry.* My guess would be that it will not. Other guesses which I have made in the past half-year have been that Al Smith would carry New York state, that St. John Ervine would be a great dramatic critic for an American newspaper, and that I would have more than twenty-six dollars in the bank on

March first. So you see my confidence in my judgment is scarcely what it used to be.

The book concerns Samuel Dodsworth, inhabitant of Zenith, maker of the Revelation automobile, and millionaire. But he is not a Babbitt, his author points out in just those words. (Now why is it that one experiences slight squirms of discomfort when Mr. Lewis, as he does several times in *Dodsworth*, uses "Babbitt" as a descriptive term? It is his own word, Heaven knows; he has seen it firmly fastened to the language, has heard it applied, perhaps a bit too easily, a million times. It is undeniable that no one has a better right to use it than has he. And yet, somehow, one's deeper respect must always go to the writer—or the grocer or the friend or the stock-broker or the tragedian —who stops just this side of doing those things that no one has a better right to do.)

Well, at any rate, Dodsworth is fifty or so, to his wife's forty-one; their two children are grown up, and no longer in need of them. So he gives up business, and he and his wife embark on a prolonged holiday abroad, to relax, to broaden, and to absorb. Surely, if Mr. Lewis in outlining his plot to some friend, had only said, "Stop me if you've heard this," more than two hundred pages of *Dodsworth* need never have been written.

The greater part of the book seems to me dull with a long and wide and thick heaviness. Mr. Lewis has been a veritable sailor in his prodigality of words. He has given all his characters far too rich a gift of utterance. For weeks, it seems, they argue the relative merits of the old world and the new; no one ever falters, no one ever searches for a phrase, no one, God help us all, ever stops.

When Mr. Lewis's ideas—for you feel, too surely, that they are Mr. Lewis's own, and not those of his characters—are not set down in the form of debates, they are given as long mental monologues of Dodsworth's. Dodsworth's thoughts come with a curious neatness, an admirable roundness of style; he broods in such apt sentences as "travel consists in perpetually finding new things that you have to do if you're going to be respectable." It is obvious that Mr. Lewis likes his main figure, and expects his reader to sympathize with the man's seekings and bafflements. But it is difficult to give tenderness to one who muses in epigrams.

And then, after all those pages and pages and pages, Dodsworth and those near to him seem to come sharply and suddenly alive. Mr. Lewis spares his words, and spends his emotions. Dodsworth's wife leaves him for a young German nobleman; the husband's dull agony and wild bewilderment, his poor, clumsy tries at finding an anodyne in little lively ladies, make a line of gripping, deep-drawn pictures. At last there is the Other Woman—the one who can give him calm and sweetness and companionship; and then there is the inevitable return of the pretentious she-dog of a wife. He goes back with her to their hopeless quarrelling, but he is a stronger man for having known beauty, and the book ends with his return to the woman who gave it to him—ends on a phrase bitter, and troubling, and cruelly deep in its knowledge.

So there you are, or, rather, there I am, in regard to *Dodsworth*. May Heaven help you, as it assisted me, through the travelogues, the debates, and the grotesquely over-drawn figures that clutter it—Mr. Lewis, who never was one to lay himself open to charges of subtilty, here frequently runs over into the realm of comic valentines. But there is that last part, to make up for the rest. You really can't know, until you have managed the first two-thirds, how high that goes in praise.

March 16, 1929

Hero Worship

Round Up—and if there were ever a cup given
for the most unfortunate title of the year, it would
be resting at this very moment upon the Ring
Lardner mantelpiece—is a collection of the pre-
viously published short stories of a great artist.
There are two classes of people whom it is my
cross to meet in my small daily round: those who
think that Ring Lardner is a humorist, and those
who have just discovered that Ring Lardner is
something more than a humorist—the latter group
makes me perhaps a shade sicker than the former.
There is hope that the Literary Guild's wide dis-
tribution of these stories, written over a period
of years, may not only serve to establish Ring
Lardner in his place, but to put all the head-
patters in theirs. If it doesn't, I shall have to go
around shooting people again, and I had more
or less retired from that line of work.

Round Up bears on its dust-cover sound and
dignified appreciation for the author from
Mencken, Edmund Wilson, and Dr. Carl Van
Doren. And Sir James Barrie lights there, like
Tinker Bell, to add: "Congratulations to Ring
Lardner. He is the real thing." It is indeed high
time to render "congratulations to Ring Lardner";

time so high as to be positively gamey. For one cannot help recalling that when "Some Like Them Cold" (to my mind, Lardner's masterpiece) was published, Edward J. O'Brien listed it in his *Best Short Stories* for that year without even one of his trick stars to signify distinction; and that the exquisite "Golden Honeymoon" was turned down by the noted editor of a famous weekly—which act should send the gentleman down to posterity along with that little band whose members include the publisher who rejected *Pride and Prejudice,* the maid who lighted the hearth with the manuscript of Carlyle's *French Revolution,* and Mrs. O'Leary's cow.

¶ It is difficult to review these spare and beautiful stories; it would be difficult to review the Gettysburg address. What more are you going to say of a great thing than that it is great? You could, I suppose, speak of Ring Lardner's unparalleled ear and eye, his strange, bitter pity, his utter sureness of characterization, his unceasing investigation, his beautiful economy. Or you could, as has been done, go in for comparing him with Ernest Hemingway and Sherwood Anderson. But it seems to me that Lardner's qualities are not to be listed but to be felt, as you read his work. And it also seems that there is no reason for comparison with Anderson and Hemingway. True, they are all writers of short stories (although, if you will kindly keep off those bolts of lightning that are just getting all set to strike me, it is my conviction that only his production of "I'm a Fool" passes Mr. Anderson into such high company), but, in the words of our hero, what of it? It is not clear to me why Ring Lardner need be compared to anybody. And may Heaven help those short-story writers who are compared to him.

April 27, 1929

¶ MRS. O'LEARY'S COW, in the legend of the times, kicked over the lamp that started the great Chicago fire of 1871.

Home Is the Sailor

Maybe you think I was just out in the ladies' room all this time, but there isn't a word of truth in it. In case the question ever comes up, I was in Switzerland, that's where I was. It seems that there was some novel notion of Getting Away from It All, coupled with a wistful dream of Trying to Forget. And when the day comes that you have to tie a string around your finger to remind yourself of what it was you were forgetting, it is time for you to go back home.

The Swiss are a neat and an industrious people, none of whom is under seventy-five years of age. They make cheeses, milk chocolate, and watches, all of which, when you come right down to it, are pretty fairly unnecessary. It is all true about yodelling and cowbells. It is, however, not true about St. Bernard dogs rescuing those lost in the snow. Once there was something in the story; but, what with the altitude and the long evenings and one thing and another, the present dogs are of such inclinations that it is no longer reasonable to send them out to work, since they took to eating the travelers. Barry, the famous dog hero, credited with the saving of seven lives, is now on view, stuffed; stuffed, possibly, with the travelers he did not bring home. Skiing is extremely difficult, and none of my affair. The most frequent accident, among ski-jumpers, is the tearing off of an ear. The edelweiss is a peculiarly unpleasant-looking flower. During the early summer, the natives fling themselves into the sport of watching one cow fight another cow; the winning lady is hung with blossoms and escorted, by her fans, from café to café, all night long. There is a higher consumption of alcohol, per capita, in Switzerland than in any other country in Europe (although there may be some slight change in those figures, now that your correspondent has returned to Tony's). The country itself is extravagantly beautiful, and practically crawling with lakes and mountains. And, while we are on that subject, how are you fixed for mountains, anyway? Because, after a year in the Alps, I should be glad to give them to you for your birthday, and throw in a mandolin.

End, and none too soon, of travelogue. But I just wanted to show you I really have been in Switzerland.

God keep me from chauvinism, but New York is beautiful. Oh, this is a lovely city you have here! I think that your skyline is astounding, and that your women are the most attractive in the world, but that there is a certain amount of exaggeration in the report that your men think of nothing but business, business, business, all the time. If it is true, then wherever *did* I get these bruises on my neck?

But there is a catch to home-coming. Welcome is surely warmer than brandy to the heart, yet there is something a little sinister in the eagerness of those people up at that bank of mine to catch a sight of, and, even, to lay a hand upon, the returned voyager. It isn't, I feel, the gesture of real friendship; there is something either a little more or a little less than that behind it. It is true that I have been wearing a catcher's mask ever since I sent out those last cheques; but what of that? Must they think of nothing but money? Can they set no value upon imagination? Surely that one cheque—numbered XXX—which I made out for three hundred and eighty-six dollars had more of pure fantasy than ever Barrie knew. But they don't care. Not they. It is not agreeable, when you wake in the night, to reflect that you have been dealing for years with an entirely material trust company. Why, those have been virtually the best years of my life, too. Just for this, just for this one thing, I hope they have a run on their old bank. The minute I finish this piece, I am going out and start a lot of dirty rumors.

Unfortunately, until then there is work to be done. When your bank account is so overdrawn that it is positively photographic, steps must be taken. Here, before I am cold off the boat, before —well, I was going to say "before I am used to American money again," but I never was used to it, really, so the phrase rather loses force— before, at any rate, I have shaken the Tauchnitz novels out of my shoes, I have to go to work. I have to write a book review. A hell of a welcome that is, I must say. A person was a fool ever to have got down off that Alp.

For I haven't, you see, been doing much reading while you had your backs turned. I am not quite ashamed of the fact. Reading, according to

Bacon—and if it wasn't Bacon, you will correct me, won't you, you big stiffs?—reading makes a full man; but to achieve the same end, I know a trick worth two of it. It is, nevertheless, somewhat appalling to return to what may be loosely called God's Country and find that my friends, all three of them, are saturated with literature, and are running around like hot cakes, reporting in considerably more words than it takes to tell it on the works they claim to have devoured. I am at just that interesting age where I cannot keep out of things. I, too, must be in the know; I, too, must quote and sigh and nod wisely. You know yourself that I cannot, in a week, do book by book what they have done. But it has been my fortune to have all literature brought to me at one crack.

The crack in question comes in two volumes— two good, thick, close-printed volumes. I can hardly bear to part with the title, for once that is out, there goes the whole review. But I shall steel myself, and give it you. The work is scattered by the *Christian Herald* (Louis Klopsch, publisher, Bible House, New York), and it is called *Forty Thousand Sublime and Beautiful Thoughts.* Yes, sir, *Forty Thousand Sublime and Beautiful Thoughts.* It is compiled by a Mr. Charles Noel Douglas, before this a stranger to me, and he has, out of his generosity, not been content with his title; barging on into the practically drunken-sailor stages of lavishness, he has shot the works on an explanatory note, printed, and appropriately, in the red. It runs: "Gathered from the Roses, Clover Blossoms, Geraniums, Violets, Morning Glories, and Pansies of Literature." It is not given to me, as it has been to Mr. Douglas, to discern who are the roses, clover blossoms, geraniums, violets, and morning glories of litera-ture. But I can say, from what I learn by getting around, that the pansies are splendidly represented. Pansies—that's for remembrance.

I tried, for my first duty is toward you, to check up on Mr. Douglas. I wanted to see if there were really forty thousand sublimes and beautifuls for you. Unhappily, it was like counting those sheep over that fence; before I had listed the first hundred I was safely asleep. But I did come upon one page that gave me a little thought, and a shade of distrust toward Mr. Douglas and even toward Mr. Louis Klopsch, of Bible House. On page four-thirty-two of the first volume, in the division of sublimes and beautifuls ranking under the head of "Death"—for Mr. Douglas has thoughtfully categoried all the thoughts alphabetically—there is Shelley's "How wonderful is Death, Death and his brother Sleep!" Then comes a quotation from Horace, one from Young, one from Marcus Antoninus. Then follows, from Shelley, "How wonderful is Death, Death and his brother Sleep!" I do not know how often such little slip-ups occur in the volumes, but having noted this one, I fear the title must be amended to "Thirty-nine Thousand Nine Hundred and Ninety-nine Sublime and Beautiful Thoughts." And that is probably big.

Mr. Douglas, as I have said, has listed his subjects alphabetically, and then collected his garden flowers to enlarge upon them. Thus, were you ever hard up for sublime thoughts upon Arbor Day or Cornerstone Laying or Heraldry or Grant's Birthday or Fish or Dimples or Agriculture (one of the sublime thoughts under "Agriculture" is: "Methinks I have a great desire to a bottle of hay; good hay, sweet hay, hath no fellow") or Aches or Corporations or Aversion (and under "Aversion" comes, sublimely and beautifully, this: "I do not like thee, Doctor Fell . . ."), all you have to do is turn to Mr. Douglas's index, and then go ahead.

You will possibly notice that the allusions, in this fascinating composition, go no further than the "H"s. There is a second volume, but, conscientious though I be, I am but flesh and blood. Up to the "H"s will hold me, Mr. Douglas and Mr. Klopsch.

Now can I go back and talk some more about Switzerland? Oh, I see. No, it doesn't matter at all. Of course I don't mind. But there was no harm in asking, was there?

January 24, 1931

¶ "Tauchnitz" designated a series of paperback books, including books in English, published in Germany and widely distributed on the Continent long before paperbacks as we know them today were published in the United States. They were much sought after by American travelers abroad but could not be legally imported because of copyright restrictions.

Kiss and Tellegen

¶ Mr. Lou Tellegen has recently seen fit to write his memoirs; and, though it is at least debatable that it would have been more public-spirited of him to have sent the results to the zoo, he has caused them to be bound within costly blue covers, and has entitled them *Women Have Been Kind*. After reading the work, or, indeed, after reading only some of it, it is borne home that the name is the most gentlemanly of understatements. "Kind" is but a feeble word for what the girls have been to Mr. Tellegen. It could have been only his chivalry that held him back from stronger terms; for you will see that he is one who carries chivalry to the point of fanaticism. You do not even have to open the book to find out that—it can be learned from the note on the dust-cover. This runs: "In recalling past love affairs, etc., Mr. Tellegen prefers to use fictitious names in cases where the lady is still alive, although the facts will be accurate." Surely one must applaud that spirit in the gentleman, and none does so more heartily than I. Only, after reading the accounts of the "love affairs, etc.," one is given to pondering how strange it is that there *are* "cases where the lady is still alive." Mr. Tellegen, Mr. Telle-

gen—I'm afraid there's been soldiering somewhere.

The blurb on the dust-cover announces, with
rather more than the usual bang, that "here are
the intimate reminiscences of the man who was
called 'the perfect lover.' " (It is not stated who
gave him this name, but I feel, somehow, that I
have guessed. I won't say yes, nor I won't say no,
but if you were to whisper to me your conjecture
that the phrase-coiner's initials are L. T., I might
admit that you were, like the countless heroines
of *Women Have Been Kind,* getting warm.) "Mr.
Tellegen's life," the blurb goes breathlessly on,
"has been, in every sense of the word, an adven-
ture." (What, one wonders, are those other senses
of the word?) "By turn actor, artist, baker, bull-
fighter, gambler, model, pugilist, prospector"
(How come, again one wonders, that he never
took up soccer?), "Mr. Tellegen has lived more
romance than others read of, and his memoirs
are as exciting as a score of novels." (I shall not
dispute that last statement, providing the publishers will let me name the score in question.)
"His frankness is thoroughly refreshing, and in
these reminiscences he has spared no one." And
that, Heaven knows, is no blurb-writer's fantasy;
indeed Mr. Tellegen has spared no one, including,
or, in fact, beginning with, the reader.

The book proper—and that adjective achieves
an almost historical distinction as an example of
unhappy selection—is written in a style that has
all the elegance of a quirked little finger and all
the glitter of a pair of new rubbers. Mr. Tellegen's
English is of the fanciest persuasion; it even includes such refinements as the exquisite participle

"gotten." It develops, by the way, that the gentleman is no slouch as a linguist. He has French, Flemish, Dutch, and Portuguese right where he wants them. But Russian, alas, threw him. Although he embarked on a nice long jaunt with a lady called Sonia, and she did everything she could, he confesses that "to this day I know only one word of Russian." The word, as one can doubtless go without saying, must have been "*da.*"

Mr. Tellegen's childhood was not a happy one. He was brought up by a somewhat unnecessarily strict tutor, who taught him, among other things, "the art of the rapier." (Thank God for that little letter "i"!) But he had such good fun, and so frequently, in after years that he surely cannot grudge the brief gray span of his youth. For at fifteen he started out, and from then on he had no dull moments. It was when he was fifteen that he set out with Sonia. The lady was not, strictly speaking, in the market at the time; she was, in fact, the girl-friend of Mr. Tellegen's father. "My father," he explains, "never forgave me for the outrage." Yet it might seem that the older Tellegen was of a nature that magnified an offense. For Sonia appears to have been a young woman that many a man would have been proud and happy to have had lifted from his life. "She conceived," Lou Tellegen says, "the rather eccentric idea of traveling in man's attire." Surely the thing for any right-thinking man to have done would have been to have presented the abductor of a young lady of any such rather eccentric ideas with a suitably inscribed silver trophy, and kissed him on both cheeks.

After Sonia, Mr. Tellegen went from love to love with a speed that sets the reader's reason to tottering. How on earth he ever found time for his other pursuits cannot be figured, even though he sets them down chronologically. He was a baker, and he was a circus performer, and he was a model for Rodin and lesser, and he was a sculptor himself, and he was a prizefighter, and he was an actor, and he wrote plays, and he spent a half-year in the South American jungle, and he gambled night and day, and he perfected a technique of self-defense by knife-throwing. Yet these things were but incidents. His life has been, first and always, the ladies—those women who have been kind to the point of sappiness. Well, I suppose that's what we all want to hear about. Nobody is much interested in the careers of bakers or playwrights.

It is a strange thing that for a few pages Lou Tellegen's book gives out a glamour. That is when he writes of Isadora Duncan (though, while we're up, I cannot recall, can you, any mention of him in her memoirs?). It seems to be impossible for any writer, no matter how bad—and goodness knows some of the worst in the world have had a crack at it—to speak of that woman without conveying something of greatness. Resent though one does the constant exhuming, and by dirty little hands, of those beautiful bones, there is always grandeur there. . . .

His account of his American tour with Sarah Bernhardt is, in a word, terrible. You get no bit of her quality; the author is too much occupied with his own concerns at the time. They were not, in another word, interesting. Nor is there much to the story of his stretch of time with Geraldine Farrar. (Miss Farrar was not his first wife, nor, so much as I can figure out events, his second or third. There came a time when it was drawn, somehow, to Mr. Tellegen's attention that gentlemen sometimes married ladies, and from then on he became a regular marryin' fool.) He is too careful about being courteous to Miss Farrar to give much realism to the record.

In all his descriptions of the great, it is the great, with that one mighty exception, who suffer. You see them all only in their relation to the escapades of Mr. Tellegen, and Mr. Tellegen's escapades are of a certain sameness. True, toward the middle of the book, there is the sprightly account of a sudden home-coming of a husband, when Mr. Tellegen was, shall we say, visiting a lovely lady in her apartment in Venice; and the distinguished guest was forced first to throw his clothes out of the window and then dive out after them, into the Grand Canal. But even before and after that, things are pretty wet.

Not the least amazing bit of the book is the postscript by Eve Casanova, the present Mrs. Tellegen. She likes him, it seems—and surely any such bad writing as her afterword must be sincere —fine. She says, among stronger things, that "he is the true type all women adore—a lover who pursues!" That has made me a little thoughtful. Maybe we both, Mr. Tellegen and I, have been giving too much credit. Maybe it isn't so kind of women to fall for a type like that. Maybe it is not kindness but gratitude. "A lover who pursues"— oh, think what that sounds like to one whose

eyes have so often rested on the ugliest modern
gesture: that of a man looking at his wristwatch!

February 21, 1931

¶ All that needs to be added to what this tells us about Lou
Tellegen is that he was a well-known actor in his time, and
that Geraldine Farrar was one of the first famous
American-born sopranos at the Metropolitan Opera. Her
female admirers were known as "Gerryflappers."

Two Lives
and Some Letters

¶ "There was no one further from sadness than Henri Gaudier," Ford Madox Ford once wrote, "whether in his being or his fate. He had youth, he had grace of person and of physique, he had a great sense of the comic. He had friendships, associates in his work, loves, the hardships that help youth. He had genius and he died a hero. Who could ask for more? Who could have better things?"

There was no resisting this setting down of Ford's words, for their beauty. But I think that there is more of music than of truth in them. "He had genius and he died a hero"—that is sure. But could there be written a sentence more compact of tragedy?

And it is evident from the letters of Henri Gaudier-Brzeska that he could have asked for more. He could have asked, and he did ask, for tenderness and for understanding. He had friendships, but they were violent and tortured and they smashed to their endings; it was his curse that calmer relations were impossible for him. Of his associates in his work he had those doubts of the man whose fevered faith is all in himself; there buzzed in his mind strange, sly noises that he took for the whisperings of a world in conspiracy against him. I know of his life only from the fine biography that stands before me, and his loves are not there listed, so I cannot say as to them. Yet it would seem to me that in that very plural lie anguish and defeat. And those "hardships that help youth" were so small and dirty and incessant that there could be no stimulus in them. That there is no sadness in his fate, I feel; for it is not his tragedy, nor anybody's, to die young. But in his being, I think indeed he could have had better things.

His letters form a part of this new book by H. S. Ede, who has held himself back from praises and from evaluations, and has not once indulged in the coquetries of the modern biographical manner. He consulted diaries and collected letters, marshalled his facts, and set down, in the dignity of simple English, the story of a star-crossed artist. I am told that it is largely due to the efforts of Mr. Ede, who is curator of the Tate Gallery in London, that the drawings and sculptures of Gaudier-Brzeska have become widely known; that his enthusiasm stands back of the artist's posthumous fame. But his book is not soiled by propaganda, nor sicklied by hero-worship. He had a wild, sad story to tell, and so he has told it. He has a fine book.

But he has, to this reader's unease and bewilderment, entitled it *Savage Messiah*. I can only conclude that the names of many of the new books are arrived at by a species of parlor game. You write down, each on a neat slip of paper, all the

nouns you can think of. Then you put them in a
hat. On an equal number of paper slips, you write
all the adjectives you ever knew; these you heap
in another hat. Then you get some innocent party
to plunge his left hand into one hat and his right
into the other, and to grasp tightly one slip in
each. Then he must pull out his clenched hands,
and be made to relinquish the papers. These are
laid next to each other, and there you have your
title. But of course, my idea of the procedure is
the purest guess-work. Possibly they don't use
hats at all; maybe it's baskets.

Savage Messiah, which is published by Knopf,
begins with the meeting in a Paris library of
Henri Gaudier and Sophie Brzeska. She was reading German, to some indefinite end, and he was
studying anatomy. He was nineteen, and she was
thirty-eight. ("The woman I love is thirty years
old," he wrote to a friend, but it was in chivalry,
not in ignorance.) She was badly battered by life
and love, and fairly started along the road to the
madhouse where she was to die. But he found her
beautiful, and so, from her photograph, she was.
They were both sick and starved and lonely. They
found each other and they lived together, though
in no closer physical communion than that im-
posed by the crowded rooms of the poor, until
five years later when, in 1915, he went out to the
War to be killed.

Mr. Ede has concerned himself, save for a quick
blocking-in of the background of each, with the
story of the life together of this woman and this
man. It is the record of a strange and sorrowful
relationship. There was no medium to it—there

were nothing but shrieking quarrels and florid reconciliations; eternally the irresistible temperament met the immovable ego. "I will be a mother to you," she offered, at their meeting, and she called him "Little Son," but it was he who was maternal toward her. He cared for her and worried over her and cheered her. His beautiful letters to her in her absences—she was often away, searching for health and writing on a lavishly conceived trilogy with which she was to stun the world—have a tenderness that squeezes the throat. It was he who put into their life together any glory and gallantry that it had.

They went to live in London, the Polish woman and the French boy; he added her name to his, and they proclaimed themselves brother and sister. In the quick years there, he did his life work. He sold an occasional drawing—during one stretch of their most horrible poverty, he went from public-house to public-house, making sketches, for pennies—but it was sculpture that he loved. ("You will have noticed," he wrote, "that civilizations begin with sculpture and end with it.") His letter announcing to a friend his dedication to his art—"I have put by the brushes and tubes and have snatched the chisel and the boaster, two simple instruments which so admirably second the most wonderful of modeling tools, the human thumb"—is written in high rapture. All his letters, indeed, have about them a clear, bright excitement. In much too long a time, I have read nothing so stirring.

They met many of the famous in London, but friendships were too difficult for them. Brzeska was hysterical, at best, and always wild with jealousy, and the boy was no easy companion. An acquaintance wrote of him, with "his long front hair hanging in a string down the side of his white brow," as "throwing his future and his past and his passion into any discussion." His need for companionship was so great that when he was asked for an evening's visit he could not bear to leave; he had to be invited, with lessening delicacy as the night waned, please to go home. So he was not asked again, and another friendship was over just as it might have been beginning.

One of the most absorbing chapters of the book is the account of the swift and turbulent acquaintanceship of the two foreigners with Katherine Mansfield and her husband, Middleton Murry, who were then editing a magazine called *Rhythm*. The affair started on the loftiest plane—"with rich hand-shakes, we swore eternal friendship"—but the ladies were difficult, Gaudier-Brzeska started throwing his future and his past and his passion into things again, and poor dear Mr. Murry, one gathers, was bewildered and a trifle scared. Possibly those handshakes were too rich; at any rate, they did not endure, and the eternal friendship ended, with a crash, in a blazingly dramatic letter from the artist to Murry, with whom, he said, he "still sympathized as a poor boy, chased by the Furies."

Recommendations seem to me always impudent; but perhaps I know you well enough to ask a favor of you. Please, will you put down whatever that thing is that you're doing and read *Savage Messiah?* It is no fun, but, if only for the sake of the letters it contains, it is a great book. And you don't get "great" out of me for red apples.

March 14, 1931

¶ HENRI GAUDIER (1891–1915), the French Vorticist sculptor, was a hero of Ezra Pound and the Vorticist school of writers; his name was unknown to most readers when *Savage Messiah* was published. . . . For KATHERINE MANSFIELD and JOHN MIDDLETON MURRY, see note for page 4.

Oh, Look—
A Good Book!

It seems to me that there is entirely too little screaming about the work of Dashiell Hammett. My own shrill yaps have been ascending ever since I first found *Red Harvest,* and from that day the man has been, God help him, my hero; but I talked only yesterday, I forget why, with two of our leading booksy folk, and they had not heard of that volume, nor had they got around to reading its better, *The Maltese Falcon.*

It is true that Mr. Hammett displays that touch of rare genius in his selection of undistinguished titles for his mystery stories—*The Maltese Falcon* and *The Glass Key,* his new one, sound like something by Carolyn Wells. It is true that had the literary lads got past those names and cracked the pages, they would have found the plots to be so many nuisances; confusing to madness, as in *Red Harvest*; fanciful to nausea, as in *The Maltese Falcon*; or, as in the case of the newly published *The Glass Key,* so tired that even this reviewer, who in infancy was let drop by a nurse with the result that she has ever since been mystified by amateur coin tricks, was able to guess the identity of the murderer from the middle of the book. It is true that he has all the mannerisms of

Hemingway, with no inch of Hemingway's scope nor flicker of Hemingway's beauty. It is true that when he seeks to set down a swift, assured, well-bred young woman, he devises speeches for her such as are only equalled by the talk Mr. Theodore Dreiser compiled for his society flapper in *An American Tragedy*. It is true that he is so hard-boiled you could roll him on the White House lawn. And it is also true that he is a good, hell-bent, cold-hearted writer, with a clear eye for the ways of hard women and a fine ear for the words of hard men, and his books are exciting and powerful and—if I may filch the word from the booksy ones—pulsing. It is difficult to conclude an outburst like this. All I can say is that anybody who doesn't read him misses much of modern America. And hot that sounds!

Dashiell Hammett is as American as a sawed-off shotgun. He is as immediate as a special extra. Brutal he is, but his brutality, for what he must write, is clean and necessary, and there is in his work none of the smirking and swaggering savageries of a Hecht or a Bodenheim. He does his readers the infinite courtesy of allowing them to supply descriptions and analyses for themselves. He sets down only what his characters say, and what they do. It is not, I suppose, any too safe a recipe for those who cannot create characters; but Dashiell Hammett can and does and has and, I hope, will. On gentle ladies he is, in a word, rotten; but maybe sometime he will do a novel without a mystery plot, and so no doggy girls need come into it. But it is denied us who read to have everything, and it is little enough to let him have his ladies and his mysteries, if he will give us such characters as Sam Spade, in *The Maltese Falcon,* and such scenes as the beating-up of Ned Beaumont in *The Glass Key.*

His new book, *The Glass Key,* seems to me nowhere to touch its predecessor. Surely it is that Beaumont, the amateur detective of the later story, a man given perhaps a shade too much to stroking his moustache with a thumbnail, can in no way stack up against the magnificent Spade, with whom, after reading *The Maltese Falcon,* I went mooning about in a daze of love such as I had not known for any character in literature since I encountered Sir Launcelot when I hit the age of nine. (Launcelot and Spade—ah well, they're pretty far apart, yet I played Elaine to both of them, and in that lies a life-story.) The new book, or, indeed, any new book, has no figure to stand near Sam Spade, but maybe all the matter is not there. For I thought that in *The Glass Key* Mr. Hammett seemed a little weary, a little short of spontaneous, a little dogged about his simplicity of style, a little determined to make startling the ordering of his brief sentences, a little concerned with having his conclusion aproach the toughness of the superb last scene of *The Maltese Falcon.* But all that is not to say that *The Glass Key* is not a good book and an enthralling one, and the best you have read since *The Maltese Falcon.* And if you didn't read that, this is the swiftest book you've ever read in your life.

April 25, 1931

¶ CAROLYN WELLS (1869–1942), the popular mystery writer, used a detective named Fleming Stone in her somewhat ladylike stories. . . . BEN HECHT (1893–1964), the journalist, novelist, and playwright, collaborated with Charles McArthur on the play *The Front Page.* Two of his novels, *Count Bruga* and *A Jew in Love,* lampooned his fellow novelist MAXWELL BODENHEIM (1893–1954), author of *Naked on Roller Skates,* who had lampooned Hecht in his *Ninth Avenue.*

Words, Words, Words

There are times when images blow to fluff, and comparisons stiffen and shrivel. Such an occasion is surely at hand when one is confronted by Dreiser's latest museum piece, *Dawn*. One can but revise a none-too-hot dialectic of childhood; ask, in rhetorical aggressiveness, "What writes worse than a Theodore Dreiser?"—loudly crow the answer, *Two* "Theodore Dreisers"; and, according to temperament, rejoice at the merciful absurdity of the conception, or shudder away from the thought.

The reading of *Dawn* is a strain upon many parts, but the worst wear and tear fall on the forearms. After holding the massive volume for the half-day necessary to its perusal (well, look at that, would you? "massive volume" and "perusal," one right after the other! You see how contagious Mr. D.'s manner is?), my arms ached with a slow, mean persistence beyond the services of aspirin or of liniment. I must file this distress, I suppose, under the head of "Occupational Diseases"; for I could not honestly chalk up such a result against "Pleasure" or even "Improvement." And I can't truly feel that *Dawn* was worth it. If I must have aches, I had rather gain them in the first tennis of the season, and get my back into it.

This present Dreiser book is the record of its author's first twenty years. It requires five hundred and eighty-nine long, wide, and closely printed pages. Nearly six hundred sheets to the title of *Dawn;* God help us one and all if Mr. Dreiser ever elects to write anything called "June Twenty-first"!

The actual account of the writer's early life, and of the lives of his mother, his father, and his nine brothers and sisters which colored and crossed it, is wholly absorbing; but, if I may say so, without that lightning bolt coming barging in the window, what honest setting-down of anyone's first years would not be? And Mr. Dreiser had, in addition, the purely literary good fortune to be a child of poverty—for when, in print, was the shanty not more glamorous than the salon?

Nor should I cavil at the length, and hence the weight, of the book, were it all given over to memories, since if a man were to write down his remembrances and his impressions up to the age of five, much less of twenty, six hundred pages could not begin to contain them. But I do fret, through *Dawn,* at the great desert patches of Mr. Dreiser's moralizing, I do chafe at such monstrous bad writing as that with which he pads out his tale. I have read reviews of this book, written by those whose days are dedicated to literature. "Of course," each one says airily, "Dreiser writes badly," and thus they dismiss that tiny fact, and go off into their waltz-dream. This book, they cry, ranks well beside the *Confessions* of Rousseau; and I, diverted, as is ever the layman, by any plump red herring, mutter, "Oh, Rousseau, my eye," and am preoccupied with that.

But on second thinking, I dare to differ more specifically from the booksie-wooksies. It is of not such small importance to me that Theodore Dreiser writes in so abominable a style. He is regarded, and I wish you could gainsay me, as one of our finest contemporary authors; it is the first job of a writer who demands rating among the great, or even among the good, to write well. If he fails that, as Mr. Dreiser, by any standard, so widely muffs it, he is, I think, unequipped to stand among the big.

For years, you see, I have been crouching in corners hissing small and ladylike anathema of Theodore Dreiser. I dared not yip it out loud, much less offer it up in print. But now, what with a series of events that have made me callous to anything that may later occur, I have become locally known as the What-the-Hell Girl of 1931. In that, my character, I may say that to me Dreiser is a dull, pompous, dated, and darned near ridiculous writer. All right. Go on and bring on your lightning bolts.

Of the earlier Dreiser, the author of *Sister Carrie* and *Jennie Gerhardt,* the portrayer of Muldoon and of Paul Dresser, in *Twelve Men,* you don't think I could be so far gone as to withhold all the reverent praise that is in me, do you? But then I read all those hundreds of thousands of words that made up *An American Tragedy* and, though I hung upon some of them, I later read the newspaper accounts of the Snyder-Gray case, and still later, of the cornering by a hundred or so of New York's finest of the nineteen-year-old

"Shorty" Crowley. And I realized, slowly and sadly, that any reporter writes better and more vividly than the man who has been proclaimed the great reporter. It is a quite fair comparison. Mr. Dreiser, with the Chester Gillette case, had a great story; the unnamed men of the daily and the evening papers with the tales of the unhappy Ruth Snyder and the bewildered Judd Gray, and the little Crowley boy who never had a prayer—they had fine stories, too. But they would have lost their jobs, had they written too much.

The booksy ones, with that butterfly touch of theirs, flutter away from Dreiser's bad writing and but brush their wings over the admission that he possesses no humor. Now I know that the term "sense of humor" is dangerous (there's a novel idea!) and that humor is snooted upon, in a dignified manner, by the lofty-minded. Thus Professor Paul Elmer More raises a thin and querulous pipe in his essay on Longfellow—I think it is—to say that there were those who claimed that Longfellow had no humor—of whom I am the first ten. All right, suppose he hadn't, he says, in effect; humor may be all very well for those that like it ("Only fools care to see," said the blind man), but there's no good making a fetish of it. I wouldn't for the world go around making fetishes; yet I am unable to feel that a writer can be complete without humor. And I don't mean by that, and you know it perfectly well, the creation or the appreciation of things comic. I mean that the possession of a sense of humor entails the sense of selection, the civilized fear of going too far. A little humor leavens the lump, surely, but it does more than that. It keeps you, from your respect for the humor of others, from making a dull jackass of yourself. Humor, imagination, and manners are pretty fairly interchangeably interwoven.

Mr. Theodore Dreiser has no humor.

I know that Mr. Dreiser is sincere, or rather I have been told it enough to impress me. So, I am assured, is Mrs. Kathleen Norris sincere; so, I am informed, is Mr. Zane Grey sincere; so, I am convinced, was Mr. Horatio Alger—whose work, to me, that of Mr. Dreiser nearest approximates—sincere. But I will not—oh, come on with your lightning again!—admit that sincerity is the only thing. A good thing, a high thing, an admirable thing; but not the only thing in letters.

The thing that most distressed me in *Dawn* was the philosophizing of its author. His is a sort of pre-war bitterness, a sort of road-company anger at conditions. Once does Mr. Dreiser quote a youthful sister: "When men proposed marriage, I found I didn't like them well enough to marry them, but when they told me I was beautiful and wanted to give me things and take me places, it was a different matter. Where I liked a man, it was easy enough to go with him—it was fun—there wasn't really anything wrong with it that I could see. Aside from the social scheme as people seem to want it, I don't even now see that it was."

On this the author comments: "At this point I am sure any self-respecting moralist will close this book once and for all!" But, you know, I must differ. I don't think that's enough to warrant the closing of a book by even the most self-respecting of moralists. I think that Mr. Dreiser believes that the world is backward, hypocritical, and mean, and so, I suppose, it is; but times have changed and Mr. D. is not now the only advanced one. I think the self-respecting moralists are much less apt to close the book "at this point" than are those that get a bit squeamish over the authenticity of a woman who says, "Aside from the social scheme as people seem to want it—"

Early in this little dandy, you saw that I had been affected by the Dreiser style. That, maybe, is responsible for this plethora of words. I could have checked all this torrent, and given you a true idea of Theodore Dreiser's *Dawn*, had I but succumbed to the influence of the present-day Nash and the sweeter-day Bentley, and had written: ¶

> Theodore Dreiser
> Should ought to write nicer.

May 30, 1931

¶ KATHLEEN NORRIS (1880–1966) was widely read as a writer of "women's fiction.". . . The famous Westerns of ZANE GREY (1875–1939), including *Riders of the Purple Sage*, are still read. . . . HORATIO ALGER (1832–1899) wrote 120 books for boys. . . . E. C. BENTLEY (1895–1956), the English versifier and mystery writer (*Trent's Last Case*), invented a form of biographical couplets called "Clerihews" after his middle name.

The Grandmother
of the Aunt
of the Gardener

Once I went through Spain, like a bat out of hell,
with a party that included—nay, grew to center
upon—a distinguished American of letters. He
spoke French as a Frenchman, rather than like
one; his German was flawless; he was persuasive
in Italian, and read Magyar for easy amusement;
but, at the hour of our start, he did not have a
stitch of Spanish to his name. Yet, when the train
clacked out of Hendaye, he began trading droll
anecdotes with the guard, and by the time we
were set in Zaragoza, he was helping the natives
along with their subjunctives. It was enough to
make me, in a word, sick.

For so lavish a gift of ear and of tongue has, to
one forever denied any part of it, something of the
repellent quality of black magic. How am I not to
be bitter, who have stumbled solo round about
Europe, equipped only with *"Non, non et non!"*
and *"Où est le lavabo des dames?"* How shall I
leash my envy, who have lived so placed that
there were weeks at a stretch when I heard or saw
no word of English; who was committed entirely
and eagerly to French manners, customs, and ab-
breviations, yet could never get it through the

head that the letter "c" on a water-faucet does not stand for "cold"?

It isn't that I have not been given every opportunity; it is simply and dismally that I am incapable of acquiring an extramural language. It is true that I can read French at glacier speed, muffing only the key-word of every sentence. It is true that I can understand it as spoken, provided the speaker is reasonably adept at pantomime. It is also, I am afraid, true that, deep in New York, there are certain spells during certain evenings—cognac is best for a starter—when my English slips from me like the shucked skin of a snake, and I converse only in the elegant French tongue. But what French! O God, O Montreal, what French! It must be faced. Struggle though I have and I do and I will, I am no darned use as a linguist. And to think that there are those, like that man of letters, to whom other languages than their own come as sweetly and as naturally as so many Springtimes is to acquire a pain in the neck for which there is no relief.

But I don't give up; I forget why not. Annually I drag out the conversation books and begin that process called brushing up. It always happens about this time, when the *Wanderlust* is as overpowering as the humidity, and I develop my yearly case of the get-away-from-it-alls. And it seems to me only the part of wisdom to dust off the Continental tongues, because you can't tell—maybe any time now one of the steamship lines will listen to reason and accept teeth instead of money, and I will be on my way back to the Old Country.

And annually I am licked right at the start.

It is happening to me even now. I have here before me a small green book called *The Ideal System for Acquiring a Practical Knowledge of French* by Mlle. V. D. Gaudel (who, in case you're going over and you don't know anyone in Paris, lives at 346 Rue Saint-Honoré). Well, everything might have been all right if Mlle. Gaudel—now why do I picture her as fond of dancing and light wines, with a way of flipping up her skirts at the back, to the cry of "Oh-la-la"?—had not subtitled her work *Just the French One Wants to Know*. Somehow, those words antagonized me, by their very blandness, so that I forgot the thirst for knowledge and searched the tome only for concrete examples of just the French one will never need. Oh-la-la, yourself, Mademoiselle, and go on and get the hell back into *La Vie Parisienne!*

Now you know perfectly well that at my time of life it would be just a dissipation of energy for me to learn the French equivalent of "Either now, or this afternoon at five." It is, at best, a matter of dark doubt that I shall ever be in any position in which it will be necessary for me to cry: "Although the captain is far from here, I always think of him." It is possible, of course, but it's a nasty wrench to the arm of coincidence that I shall find occasion for the showing-off of the phrase "Her marriage took place (*eut lieu*) on the 2nd of April, 1905"; or that it will be given me to slide gently into a conversation with "I admire the large black eyes of this orphan." Better rest I silent forever than that I pronounce: "In this case, it is just that you should not like riding and swimming"; or that I inquire: "Are you pleased that they will bring the cricket set?"; or that I swing into autobiography with the confession: "I do not like to play blindman's buff"; or that I so seriously compromise myself as to suggest: "I propose that you breakfast with me and afterwards look for our friends."

The future is veiled, perhaps mercifully, and so I cannot say that never, while I live, shall I have occasion to announce in French: "It was to punish your foster-brother"; but I know which way I would bet. It may be that some day I shall be in such straits that I shall have to remark: "The friend of my uncle who took the quill feather bought a round black rice-straw hat trimmed with two long ostrich feathers and a jet buckle." Possibly circumstances will so weave themselves that it will be just the moment for me to put in: "Mr. Fouchet would have received some eel." It might occur that I must thunder: "Obey, or I will not show you the beautiful gold chain." But I will be damned if it is ever going to be of any good to me to have at hand Mlle. Gaudel's masterpiece: "I am afraid he will not arrive in time to accompany me on the harp."

Oh, "Just the French One Wants to Know" *mon œil*, Mademoiselle. And you know what you can do, far better than I could tell you.

There is a little more comfort in a booklet called *The American in Europe*, where neat sentences are listed for use in almost every contingency. Yet, somehow there sneaked in under the curious heading of "The Theatre, the Music" this monologue: "I love you; Don't forget me; The beautiful blue eyes; Let us love one another; I play all my pieces by heart without any music." Doubtless they order

those things rather better in France, but I feel
that, according to our New York ideas, that last
phrase is all wrong. It should run, for its place
in the sequence: "Come on down to my apartment—I want to show you some remarkably fine
etchings I just bought."

To turn to Spanish proves small good. Here I
have a stamp-sized work, sent out by Hugo's Sim-
plified System, entitled *How to Get All You Want
While Travelling in Spain* (and a pretty sweeping
statement, too, Mr. Hugo, if I may say so). Mr.
Hugo has captured the Iberian spirit so cleverly
as to enable his pupils phonetically to learn "I
don't like this table—this waiter—this wine," and
to go on from there into truly idiomatic crabbing.

Mr. Hugo is good, but his book can never touch
that manual of Spanish conversation that it was
once my fortune to pick up in Madrid; though I
curse myself for leaving it there, one scene in it
is forever branded on my brain and engraved
upon my heart. The premise is that a mother and
her engaged daughter visit a furniture shop to
select the double bed (*matrimonio*) for the future bride's home. (The work was titled, as I
recall it, *Easy Conversations for Everyday Occasions*.) The mother sees a bed that she approves
—the daughter, in the Latin manner, never opens
her trap. Mom asks the salesman the price of the
piece of furniture, and he tells her, with respect,
"Thirteen pesetas." To which the dear little gray-
haired lady replies, very simply, "¡Jesú!" . . .

Well. I got a long way from the place I started.
All I meant to do was moan over my trouble in

working on foreign languages. And it took me all these words to do it. The thing to do, surely, is to give the French and the Spanish books to some deserving family, and get to work on that English.

July 25, 1931

Not Even Funny

When one had put sex carefully away on the highest cupboard-shelf, in a box marked "Winter Hats—1916," it is somewhat melancholy to read a book by Tiffany Thayer—melancholy, that is, in that no wistful memories whatever are thus evoked. Mr. Thayer, it is deplorably unnecessary to explain, has achieved great prominence in that school of American authors which may be described as the boys who ought to go regularly to a gym. He is beyond question a writer of power; and his power lies in his ability to make sex so thoroughly, graphically, and aggressively unattractive that one is fairly shaken to ponder how little one has been missing. Bewildered is the fox who lives to find that grapes beyond reach can be *really* sour.

Mr. Thayer's latest work is called, with that simplicity which is the gaudiest flower of pretentiousness, *An American Girl.* I am at a loss to comprehend why this was the selected title, since the book displays any number of American girls, all alike in seeming to be, as Henry James said of George Sand, highly accessible. Perhaps it was felt that the name established an excellent base for a superstructure of sequels—*An American Girl at Yale, An American Girl on a Gunboat,* and so forth. Or perhaps Mr. Thayer, too, sometimes nods, and simply couldn't think of another thing to call the blamed book. Only in the friendliest spirit is it suggested that for later editions he might care to change his present rather pastel title to the possibly more provocative *I Am a Fugitive from a Daisy Chain Gang.* ¶

It is not, alas, the mention of sex but that of dullness which brings up the matter of Mabel Dodge Luhan's *Background,* the entering volume of a ¶ proposed series that will comprise her *Intimate Memories.* Last year, Mrs. Luhan gave us *Lorenzo in Taos,* which seems to me one of the most valuable works of our time. It is extraordinarily well written, swift, sure, and excited; it is of enormous importance as a portrait of D. H. Lawrence; and it is in all literature the most staggering survey of the wrong things a woman will do who sets out to wrest from a man his romantic devotion. I am convinced that Mrs. Luhan had no idea of all she was revealing, nor even of what she was revealing, for no woman could knowingly so display herself and go on walking the world; and it is, I think, in that preposterous naïveté, somehow so terrible, somehow so moving, that lies the eternal value of the book.

In *Lorenzo in Taos,* Mrs. Luhan includes Lawrence's letters to her on the subject of her *Intimate Memories,* which work she had in progress during those last hopeful, heart-breaking months when he was in Italy awaiting the health that did not come. Apparently, she wrote him about her work, and she wrote him about it, and she *wrote* him about it, and finally she sent him the manuscript. Lawrence told her to publish her memoirs in the United States, but to substitute invented names for real; he told her to distribute them by private subscription; he told her to try having them published in Germany; he told her to have them printed in Paris on her own money; he told her to lock them in a safe-deposit vault for fifty years; he told her to give them, sealed, to the French Academy, to be opened after her death; he all but told her, in all but words, to tie them around her neck and go jump in the lake. So the first volume of them is now out, published by Harcourt, Brace and Company at three dollars the throw.

This book takes the author only as far as her presentation to the society of her native city of Buffalo, but it does it with unflagging attention to dusty detail. Mrs. Luhan is a woman of relentless memory, and no littlest scroll in the woodwork of any room she ever entered in her girlhood eludes her recall or her description. It may be in her forthcoming volumes, when she gets into her stride of marrying people, things will liven up a bit. But *Background* is to me as dull, and with that same stuffy, oppressive, plush-thick dullness, as an album of old snapshots of somebody else's family group.

March 18, 1933

¶ TIFFANY THAYER (1902–1959) attained wide notoriety and sales for his sex novels, daring in their day, including his own version of *The Three Musketeers*. . . . *I Am a*

Fugitive from a Georgia Chain Gang, an autobiographical book by Robert Elliott Burns, was a best seller in 1932. . . . MABEL DODGE, socialite daughter of a Buffalo automobile manufacturer, was known for her salon and her literary friends. In the D. H. Lawrence circle in Taos she met and married an Indian, Tony Luhan.

Index